THE REAPER *Essays*

THE REAPER *Essays*

By Mark Jarman
& Robert McDowell

Introduction by Meg Schoerke

STORY LINE PRESS

1996

Story Line Press
Three Oaks Farm
Brownsville, OR 97327

This publication was made possible thanks in part to the generous support
of the Nicholas Roerich Museum, the Andrew W. Mellon Foundation, the
National Endowment for the Arts, and our individual contributors.

Book design by Chiquita Babb

Library of Congress Cataloging-in-Publication Data

Jarman, Mark.
    The Reaper essays / by Mark Jarman & Robert McDowell :
introduction by Meg Schoerke.
        p.   cm.
    ISBN 1-885266-21-9 (alk. paper)
        1. American poetry—20th century—History and criticism.
    2. Poetics. I. McDowell, Robert, 1953- . II. Reaper (Santa
Cruz, Calif.) III. Title.
    PS325.J37   1996
    811'.509—dc2096-21735

                                                        CIP

The Reaper is the great deleter, the one who
determines the story's end. . . .

Contents

Introduction

As "the great deleter, the one who determines when the story ends," *The Reaper* determined when its own story would end and ceased publication in 1989. The death was not premature, for the editors, who consistently emphasized the need for narrative and stylistic limits and chastised poets for not knowing when to stop, sought to extinguish *The Reaper* at the right moment. In 1989 the right moment had come, for by then the magazine had served its purpose: to make narrative a viable option for contemporary poetry. Although narrative poetry had not disappeared during the 1960s, '70s, or even the early '80s, it had been overshadowed by confessional, deep image, and meditative poetry. By the late 1970s, a number of critics had begun to attack the excesses that they saw in contemporary poetry, but *The Reaper*'s editors were the first to propose narrative as an alternative and *The Reaper* became the only little magazine of the 1980s—even of the century—to focus on narrative poetry and to develop a sustained argument in favor of its vitality, objectives that set the magazine in the vanguard of what came to be known as "The New Narrative" movement in poetry. *The Reaper*, moreover, took a stance that was both adversarial—aimed to explode the complacency of contemporary letters—and shrewdly omniscient—some would say "holier-than-thou." Such a stance, however, was not only bracing but refreshing, since it was grounded upon the strength of editorial conviction and the sharply-honed point-of-view that readers could always expect to find in the magazine.

The Reaper's stark black and white cover illustrations reflect its uncompromising objectives and clear focus, yet also suggest the variety of moods that surface in its narrative poems and criticism, for the depictions of the grim reaper range from the domestic to the apocalyptic. The first cover, a reproduction of George Dance's "Death, The Extinguisher," plays off of the tension between these two poles: an unwary man sitting at a desk is about to be smothered by a candle-snuffer wielded by a huge skeleton who looms behind him. The drawing embodies the editors' warning in their statement of purpose, "Where *The Reaper* Stands,"—"death, which gives us only so much time to tell our story, [defines] its necessity and [makes] the choice of imagery urgent"; the drawing also sheds light on the editors' view of where they would stand in relation to the contemporary literary scene: like the skeletal reaper in Dance's picture, they would position themselves above and behind poets, editors, and critics and proclaim that "their time is running out."

And yet, like *The Reaper's* criticism, the cover art, though unsettling, is often witty as well and suggests that McDowell and Jarman had other goals in mind than mere levelling. In Gustave Dore's etching on the cover of Number 3, the reaper, descending through the clouds on an angry stallion and accompanied by a host of winged ghouls, looks oddly pregnant; the outward curve of his distended belly, thrust forward in opposition to the inward curve of his lowered scythe, serves as the focal point of the picture. The iconography attests to the dual function of the grim reaper as destroyer and creator, an agent of transformation who, though merciless, becomes the harbinger of regeneration. Likewise, *The Reaper* styled itself as both a destroyer, keen to cut down poetry afflicted by "inaccuracy, bathos, sentimentality, posturing, [and] evasion," and a creator of what the editors hoped would be a new emphasis in contemporary poetry: the regenerative power of the narrative line. In Numbers 9 and 10, the two issues that fall in the middle of the magazine's eight year tenure, the covers depict the traditional figure of the scythe-bearing reaper standing in a field; the first, an etching by Barbara Pleasant, shows a stiff, tight-lipped farmer in a cleared field, while the second, a late-nineteenth-century photograph, features a nude young woman posed among sheaves. Apart from their evocation of *The Reaper's* midwestern origins, the two covers reflect the editors' determination not only to clear away the chaff that they found in contemporary poetry, but also to cull a rich harvest between the magazine's pages.

As befitting a little magazine that championed narrative, McDowell and Jarman fashioned an editorial persona, The Reaper, who, like the main character in a good short story, developed over the years and enabled them to dramatize their concerns with vehemence and humor. The persona inspired a running series of jokes in the correspondence section of the magazine and offered the editors, letter writers, and guest essayists rich opportunities for black humor, as in the magazine's parody of public relations slogans—"Don't Be Caught Dead Without Reading It"—which appeared on the copyright page of every issue. But the persona served a deeper purpose, for it gave McDowell and Jarman the chance to temper their sharp criticisms of contemporary poetry with levity, so that their analyses of representative poems, dominant trends, and contemporary editorial practices, as well as their more succinct pronouncements, such as the list of "Non-Negotiable Demands," avoided seeming crabbed or pedantic. As they note in their checklist, "How to Write Narrative Poetry," "humor may . . . change the pace subtly, allowing the reader to reflect on what has been read and prepare for what is to come." The humor that, through the persona of The Reaper, characterized the magazine's critical essays, correspondence, and many of its cover illustrations, helped to vary *The Reaper's* pace and, in keeping with the magazine's apocalyptic tone, prepared readers for "what [was] to come": the turn toward narrative that *The Reaper* predicted would invigorate American poetry.

The checklist, "How to Write Narrative Poetry," can serve equally well as a guide to the magazine's strengths, for *The Reaper* featured not only humor and a main character, but also many of the other elements detailed on the list. Unlike many literary magazines, *The Reaper* has a clear beginning, middle, and end: In the beginning issues, the editors confidently announced their intentions; at the midpoint, in issue 10, they published Donald Hall's acute critical evaluation of the previous nine issues; and, although the last issue lacked a retrospective essay, they ended the magazine at a time when narrative was gaining recognition as an important dimension of contemporary poetry. The decision corroborates their attention in the checklist to the need for restrictions such as "compression of time" and "containment," for *The Reaper* was marked by its consistency and economy. Each critical essay followed logically from the essay in the preceding issue and explored a compelling subject. In their discussions of contemporary poetry, McDowell and Jarman concentrated on illuminating the private gestures that make or break a poem and, in their careful observation of those gestures, along with their emphasis on "a poetry that communicate[s] a vision to the reader, one that the reader can enter and share," they sought to create for their own readers "the impression of participation," both in the narrative poems discussed and in the act of criticism. Equally, in the spirit of participation, McDowell and Jarman were willing to publish essays and letters that criticized their views, which made *The Reaper* a forum for debate. But, unlike the criticism that they attack in "Navigating the Flood," which "seem[s] *not* to include the poem, but only ways of talking about the poem" and "creat[es] an exclusive audience for poetry," McDowell and Jarman's criticism gives priority to poems and envisions an inclusive, general audience for poetry. Finally, *The Reaper* fulfills the "location" requirement of the checklist, for, particularly in the poems of Jared Carter, the poet most frequently published in its pages, it "present[s an] intimate involvement with an identifiable region," rural Indiana.

The one item on the "How to Write Narrative Poetry" checklist to which *The Reaper's* critical essays do not conform is number 6, "understatement." Although the arguments are supported, for the most part, with detailed examples and analyses, the editors, in staking their claims, tend toward declamatory overstatement and prefer the rhetoric of proclamation and lofty judgment over that of compromise and empathy. And yet overstatement, in the context of *The Reaper*'s tenacious criticism, serves the same function as understatement does in narrative poetry: the device "sustains and contributes to the development of drama. Without drama there is no tension; without tension the story sags." The dramatic tension of *The Reaper*'s criticism, which springs from the editors' willingness—even eagerness—to trouble the waters, gives it a vitality and urgency that the more polite and conciliatory criticism of many other poetry journals lacks. As Donald Hall argues in "Reaping *The Reaper*" (issue Number 10), "although The Reaper's logic would not always pass Argument and Persuasion in English 101; . . . although praise may overpraise and blame overblame," *The Reaper*'s greatest strength was "its singleminded bloodymindedness." In Hall's view, *The Reaper*'s anger—which aligned it with other recent "lethal or hellish" poetry journals such as *River Styx*, *Exquisite Corpse*, and *Sulfur*—was essentially healthy, since its source was restless dissatisfaction with the status quo—a discontent which fuels good poetry.

Such discontent, and the adversarial stance to which it gave rise, also places *The Reaper* firmly in the tradition of other volatile twentieth-century little magazines such as *Blast*, the *Fifties*, and *Kayak*, whose criticism, along with attacking dominant trends that had edged over into mannerism, aimed to promote a contrary approach to writing poetry. In fact, *The Reaper*'s on-going manifesto championing narrative poetry bears comparison to Pound's Imagist manifestoes: both are notable not only for what they include, but for what they omit. Pound, in his campaign against "emotional slither" and mannered, worn-out conventions, called for a poetry that was "harder and saner" and "nearer to the bone": "it will be as much like granite as it can be, its force will lie in its truth, its interpretive power . . . ; I mean it will not try to seem forcible by rhetorical din, and luxurious riot."[1] Similarly, *The Reaper*, in objecting to contemporary poets' "sentimental disdain for accuracy," "mannered poems that rely on opaque language," and dependence on "lax lines, flaccid syntax" and "inconsequential," "pre-determined emotion," praised the granite clarity of "the narrative line and its linear simplicity" and called for "restraint in choice of language."

Pound, of course, in his early manifestoes, proposed Imagism as a solution and paid scant attention to narrative, although in his praise of the troubadours and of Browning he evinced a healthy respect for narrative poetry. McDowell and Jarman, on the other hand, in promoting narrative poetry, set themselves against what they saw as the late-century exhaustion of Imagism:

> Imagism has become enhanced; it has become speculation, moving from the thing pictured to the act of picturing itself. Not a minor difference, and one that has led to an increase in the number of words one finds in any given poem, due to the discursiveness of meditative verse. A happy reader or author might call this *fullness*; but *inflation* and *prolixity* are often appropriate descriptions, too.

Despite their complaints about the decadence of meditative poetry's Imagistic tendencies, they stress that the narrative line be upheld by "the accurate image" and that a character's private gestures be illuminated "not by proclamation but by presentation," standards which recall Pound's maxim, "Direct treatment of the 'thing' whether subjective or objective." *The Reaper*'s editors, however, in their condemnation of the solipsism that they find in contemporary poetry, tend toward exclusive emphasis on a poem's "objective" details and often seem to discount subjectivity altogether. Equally, their suspicion of rhetorical excess leads them to view complex figurative language and syntax as mere artifice, rather than seeing them as components that, if handled skillfully by a poet, can give force and

---

[1] "A Retrospect," *The Literary Essays of Ezra Pound*, ed. T. S. Eliot (New York: New Directions, 1968; originally published 1935), 12.

definition to a narrative. (The work of E. A. Robinson stands as just one example of how rhetoric can sustain narrative poetry; Robinson, too, along with Robert Frost, also fruitfully explored the extent to which a speaker's subjectivity colors and adds dynamic tension to a narrative.) Finally, in their focus on the building blocks of narrative—plot line and character development—*The Reaper's* editors don't pay sufficient attention to the musical dimensions of poetry that Pound favored so strongly. Their declaration in the Frost essay that "the story *is* the poem" is telling, for even a narrative poem should involve other elements along with a good story: the story may be the poem, but the poem is not the story alone. As Hall argues, "when The Reaper calls for narrative, I think he misdirects his attention to plot or action, which scarcely exist in Frost's 'Directive' and 'West Running Brook,'" for these poems "are surely not narrative poems at all but speeches called forth by observed circumstances; they are (like 'Thanatopsis'; like most of the best verse in America and England for the last five hundred years) meditations on experience in artful language making satisfying shapes."

The Reaper's criticism is noteworthy not only for its emphasis on narrative poetry, but for the attention it gives to the expectations of the general reader. Rather than assume that the readership of poetry is limited to an academic subculture—an inbred community of professional poets or theory-oriented critics—*The Reaper's* editors envision a broader audience attuned to poetry that explores not simply the nature and possibilities of poetry but of human experience. Through balancing a variety of methods—stern judgment, careful analysis, and satire—McDowell and Jarman aimed to resuscitate both narrative poetry and a contentious, evaluative criticism. By refusing to view poetry as merely "grist for critical mills" or to pander to varieties of contemporary poetry that seem designed primarily for critics conversant with theory, *The Reaper's* editors stressed content over what they felt was an excessive and often self-conscious preoccupation with form on the part of both poets and critics. *The Reaper's* essays, like the narrative poetry the magazine celebrated, "cast a cold eye on criticism," while at the same time exemplifying a style of criticism grounded upon "the immediate event of the poem itself."

Thus *The Reaper*'s criticism is significant not simply, as Hall argues, for its tone—its "bloodymindedness"—but because of the editors' relentless quest to offer a detailed and precise definition of narrative poetry and for the substantive questions they raise about contemporary American poetry and its criticism. These objectives, moreover, strike a firm balance, so that McDowell and Jarman's arguments about the shortcomings of the dominant, meditative style and the strength of the narrative line illuminate and reinforce one another. Throughout the 1980s, *The Reaper* provoked controversy that was—and still is—vital for the development of American poetry. Hopefully, with the publication of this anthology, that controversy will continue for a long time to come.

Meg Schoerke

THE REAPER *Essays*

Where *The Reaper* Stands

The Reaper is the great deleter, the one who determines when the story ends.

Most contemporary poets have forgotten him. Navel gazers and mannerists, their time is running out. Their poems, too long even when they are short, full of embarrassing lines that "context" is supposed to justify, confirm the suspicion that our poets just aren't listening to their language anymore. Editors and critics aren't listening much, either. Despite their best, red-faced efforts, their favorite gods—inaccuracy, bathos, sentimentality, posturing, evasion—wither at the sound of *The Reaper's* whetstone singing.

What *The Reaper* wishes to show in this its first issue are examples from current British and American poets who reject the slick and inadequate gods listed above; and in the first in a series of essays *The Reaper* takes issue with the conclusions of five of our most prominent critics (some of them poets) who met at *After the Flood*, a symposium held at the Folger Shakespeare Library in Washington, D.C. in November, 1979.

The Reaper maintains that both the accurate image and the narrative line, two determining factors of the poem's shapeliness, have been keenly honed and kept sharp by the poets included here, whereas many of their counterparts, forgetting these necessities, have wandered into a formless swamp where only the skunk cabbage of solipsistic meditation breeds, with its cloying flowers.

It is *The Reaper's* ultimate aim to drain the bog of American writing by providing a format for poems and stories that take chances and make squeamish the editors of most other literary magazines with more fashionable "tastes." The second issue will be devoted to contemporary short fiction and will explore, in a second essay, the relationship between the fiction writer and the poet.

The poems collected here in issue number one, unmannered, tell stories *which their imagery serves*. Their authors know when to stop, which acknowledges the role of *The Reaper*. They believe, in fact, in death, which gives us only so much time to tell our story, defining its necessity and making the choice of imagery urgent.

Do contemporary writers think they can wander the marshland forever? *The Reaper's* scythe is already whispering at their heels!

Navigating the Flood

In November, 1979, *The Reaper* attended After the Flood, a symposium at the Folger Shakespeare Library in Washington, D.C. where panelists Harold Bloom, Richard Howard, John Hollander, Donald Davie, Marjorie Perloff and Stanley Plumly scrutinized the state of contemporary American poetry and its criticism. During the presentations, group discussions and informal chats, the dominant emerging perspective seemed *not* to include the poem, but only ways of talking about the poem.

Richard Howard began his lecture by "accounting for the critic's encounter with the new poem." Donald Davie, promising an "alternative" to the popular poem of today, conjured Turner Cassity, "a writer of *verse*, in the sense that central to his awareness of what he is doing is the integrity of the verseline, and particularly of the value of the *turn* from one line into the next." Stanley Plumly reviewed the old argument between formalism and free verse. Marjorie Perloff lamented the lack of serious critical attention to the performance texts of David Antin and John Cage. John Hollander implied that a poem in its very form is a critical text that comments on itself. And Harold Bloom typified the symposium's spirit by quoting and misreading Oscar Wilde: "*The only civilized form of autobiography*—I know no more adequate characterization of the highest criticism."

It was remarkable to discover how little the panelists actually disagreed. *The Reaper* has come to four conclusions about the symposium topic.

1. Poetry, more than ever, is harnessed by and subordinate to its criticism.
2. Criticism grows out of an arbitrary neurotic sensibility.
3. Critics are creating an exclusive audience for poetry, which consists only of themselves and the poets they promote.
4. When critics cease with explanations and turn to examples, more often than not, what they like is not good: They try to invent surprises where no surprise exists.

The first point is certainly debatable, for poets tend (and rightfully so) to get their hackles up when accused of writing from any impulse but the desire to do the thing itself. Yet, here is John Ashbery from *As We Know*:

> It behooves
> our critics
> to make the poets more
>   aware of
> what they are doing, so that
>   poets in turn
> can stand back from their
>   work and be enchanted
>   by it
> and in this way make room
>   for the general public
> to crowd around and be
>   enchanted by it too.

This is a sorry goal for poets and critics. It does not take into consideration the possibility that the praise and instruction might be misdirected. At the symposium Ashbery was the one poet deferred to, analyzed, airbrushed, fawned over, and lovingly chided by every panelist. *The Reaper* is not saying that a living poet should not receive such praise, but he should beware of taking it seriously.

After all, the poet creates and the critic analyzes that creation. However, as became clear at the symposium, contemporary critics are not satisfied with their role. This is where the arbitrary neurotic sensibility comes in. In their anxiety to stake their own claim, to somehow thrust themselves beyond Romanticism and the New Critics, they are defensive and in a state of constant retreat. Thus the earnest attempts to define something called the "new poem." Howard's definition ran thus:

> . . . poetry released from its old subservience to repetition, a poetry in which no experience is reverted to or recuperated—a poetry of revelation, call it, when memory and apocalypse are identical. A poetry of centripetal illumination, without any of the old axiological signs and spells which served once to hold it in our minds. A poetry without charms—*carminae*. A poetry whose imagery, hugged close to the self, is often, in that repository, pulverized beyond all recognition of shared contours. A poetry without rhyme; a poetry without constants in verbal behavior; a kind of *insistent unpredictability.*"

From this description Howard sidestepped the issue by lapsing into a consideration of titles for poems (deferring to Hollander) and sloppily linked this topic to the necessity for naming things. He evoked Adam's task of naming the beasts to provide authority for this arbitrary judgment; but the *piéce de resistance* was a casserole bubbling with inaccuracy. What is more repetitive or more a part of the old axiological signs and spells than the process of naming? Wasn't Adam's task prelapsarian, before memory began? Is contemporary poetry without rhyme, without constants in verbal behavior? Who is not listening here?

Stanley Plumly, who came closest to putting forth a sustained and coherent new program for reading, had this to say:

I'm not, by the way, sponsoring a simple-minded law of contraries, in which form is supposed to act as an anchor to content, content the current trying to carry the boat out to sea. I am talking about the dialectic of form itself, an argument of the energies within a poem.

This is all well and good, but how can one talk of the dialectic with only one side—form? Isn't this a retreat from dealing with content *at all?* Furthermore, Plumly's assertion that we have begun to extend our aesthetic to include the whole length of the sentence—accurate as it is—still implies that we must invent ways of reading the poem that traditionally doesn't measure up *as poetry,* before we can even discuss its content. Finally, these criteria manifest that arbitrary sensibility with which the critic claims too much for his role. *The Reaper's* third conclusion is linked to the first and is illustrated by the critic's desire to celebrate the activity of talking about poems—not the art itself. Bloom's theory that a poem, in order to last, must provoke several strong misreadings is a brilliant though diabolical excuse for the perpetuity of criticism, for its domination over poetry. It is a theory that misses the immediate event of the poem itself and implies that the reader cannot know which poems are significant until the critic informs him. This is neither generous opinion nor sharing, but narrow judgment and dogmatic telling. In fact, in its demand for passivity, it is not far removed from Marjorie Perloff's preferences. For what is David Antin's associative monologue if it is not language and personality usurped by advertising, by amateurish videotaping, by the montage and jump-cut of the cinema, by the visual dicta of television, all of which require nothing more of the viewer than passive observation.

Passivity is the root characteristic of those who would be bought and sold. If we are not inherently passive, there is the intimidating spectre of the critic to persuade us. How close, how cozily snug, are the following, "divergent" approaches to contemporary poetry, each critic trying to make taste rather than to recognize it where it already exists. Donald Davie must "attach a minus-sign to those attributes—'personal,' 'obsessively individual,' 'idiopathic'" which are found in many contemporary poems. Predictably, he turned to poets like himself, Cassity and Robert Pinsky, all disciples of Yvor Winters, giving the distinct impression that he carried wrapped in his cloak a thin birch rod for the purpose of rapping the knuckles of any poet declining his invitation to dress in period costume. Richard Howard, propped on the seesaw opposite Davie, had this to say:

> A year in the galleys, among proofs of the new books and in the writing workshops is enough to blunt my point to murderous instrumentality: poems are written out of the acknowledged existence of other poems, poems are named out of the acknowledged existence of such writing. What they are written in, named in, remains the mystery.

Both critics seem equally frightened by the same thing, but where Davie proposes retreat, Howard recommends retrenchment. John Hollander managed to abstract his way into the middle ground.

> They (poems) are always making parables about their form, about the way in which poetry is half-created by, and half creates, its patterns and structures. Precisely put: For the true poetry, the schemes of form become trope; figures of linguistic structure become figures of thought and even of will. This is precise, from the standpoint of rhetoric. From that of poetic composition itself, we might say that where pattern was, meaning will be.

Precise, indeed—but less than accurate. *The Reaper* insists that true poetry is not rhetoric, and though ordered in its presentation, its meaning will be in spite of pattern.

Now *The Reaper* comes to the fourth conclusion which assails the preoccupation with what Howard calls "the mystery." Presumably he is talking about the poet's need for a rhetoric and the poem's need for a moment in which its language ceases to be the language of the poet. What, then, remains? The answer is simple—*artifice*, the only thing these critics are capable of recognizing and talking about.

Critics spend more time touting the sensational, the sleight-of-hand, than any style that springs from necessity. It is one way of handling the dilemma of having little to say from intuition and the heart; the critic who is interested primarily in developing a new program for reading can always babble on from the cramp of pre-digested theories. What counts is the evasive text which gives the critic the opportunity to invent substance where little exists. Poets who practice this sort of writing hide in their work and lend themselves to abstract theorization. Nothing can better indict the misdirected energy emblematic of the contemporary situation than an accurate examination of these critics' chosen beacons. *The Reaper* will proceed to pull the plug on works by two contemporary poets held up as shining examples of the "new" poetry: "Wet Casements" by John Ashbery and "Meditation at Lagunitas" by Robert Hass.

First, the Ashbery poem.

Wet Casements

> *When Eduard Raban, coming along*
> *the passage, walked into the open*
> *doorway, he saw that it was raining.*
> *It was not raining much.*
>
> Kafka, "Wedding Preparations
> in the Country"

The conception is interesting: to see, as though reflected
In streaming windowpanes, the look of others through
Their own eyes. A digest of their correct impressions of
Their self-analytical attitudes overlaid by your
Ghostly transparent face. You in falbalas
Of some distant but not too distant era, the cosmetics,
The shoes perfectly pointed, drifting (how long you
Have been drifting; how long I have too for that matter)

Like a bottle-imp toward a surface which can never be
    approached,
Never pierced through into the timeless energy of a present
Which would have its own opinions on these matters
Are an epistemological snapshot of the processes
That first mentioned your name at some crowded cocktail
Party long ago, and someone (not the person addressed)
Overheard it and carried that name around in his wallet
For years as the wallet crumbled and bills slid in
And out of it. I want that information very much today.

Can't have it, and this makes me angry.
I shall use my anger to build a bridge like that
Of Avignon, on which people may dance for the feeling
Of dancing on a bridge. I shall at last see my complete face
Reflected not in the water but in the worn stone floor of my
    bridge.
I shall keep to myself.
I shall not repeat others' comments about me.

Harold Bloom saw this poem as a "strange, late, meditative version
of the Keatsian ode, obviously not in mere form, but in rhetorical
stance." Naturally, he saw as strengths what *The Reaper* reads as weak-
nesses. For example, the "look of others through/Their own eyes"
to Bloom is "an evasion, wholly characteristic of Ashbery's self-ex-
pression through his own reflexive seeing." To *The Reaper* it is indeed
an evasion, but that it is characteristic of Ashbery is not, as Bloom
implies, a virtue.

It is necessary to differentiate between the self and emotional im-
pact in the poem. Development of character is important. This can
include the first person. A poet like Ashbery and a critic like Bloom
have overreacted in their *ouevre* of deception. They distrust the first
person as a character; indeed they distrust any character that can be
clearly identified. This distrust has created a poetry of obfuscation,

for all characters in the poem, as they represent *the poet's own emotions,* must be camouflaged. What is the result? The protective coloration of posturing and manners.

As you can see, two central characters are introduced here, "You in falbalas" and "someone (not the person addressed)." The former, as a figure of longing, could make this poem work. However, the responsibility for that longing, which is the poet's, is shrugged off on the latter character. The later introduction of "I" does not excuse this for he appears to meditate on the actions of "someone" (. . . someone (not the person addressed)/Overheard it and carried that name around in his wallet/For years. . .) as if they were not his own. In other words, "someone" covers for "I." Were we to substitute "I" for "someone" the emotional impact would be much stronger, not deflected as it is, and that in Ashbery's eyes is dangerous. So, he shirks that responsibility.

What is the consequence of this? A sentimental disdain for accuracy. The first four and a half lines show this. How can we see the look of others through their own eyes in a reflection? Is this interesting conception, which is impossible to see and therefore inaccurate, suggested by Cordelia's eyes as wet casements, by Eduard Raban's reaction to the weather? The sentimentality here is implicit in the poet's attitude. It is a poetic posture, especially when you consider the concrete image of the streaming windowpanes and the subtle reference to the cliché of seeing ourselves as others see us. It is sentimental to think that such posturing will mask inaccurate language, or that a series of abstractions ("a digest of their correct impressions of /Their self-analytical attitudes. . .") holds together as anything more than a string of meaningless words. The ghostly transparent face overlaid here is merely a bit of poetry to catch our attention.

Our attention caught, Ashbery begins to tell us a story, and that is dangerous. He risks emotion. But this story is suspended in a periodic sentence of nine lines. Between the subject and the predicate Ashbery introduces more obfuscations. "Of some distant but not too distant era, . . ." The priggishness of this phrase is self-evident. "The cosmetics, / The shoes, perfectly pointed, . . ." two details: one general, one specific, but what do they mean? Doesn't falbalas tell us enough? The parenthetical statement is an aside we never quite understand. Again we have the sentimental liaison between poet and reader. The poet assumes that the reader will be touched by the word "drifting" and the idea of time passing. Then comes the one dynamic simile in the entire poem: "Like a bottle-imp." But it is lost in gratuitous paradox, "toward a surface which can never be approached." The next two lines ("Never pierced through into the timeless energy of the present / Which would have its own opinions on these matters") are an example of Ashbery's strongest suit, tone. The tonal shift is witty. The inflated rhetoric of "the timeless energy of a present" is pierced by the clever idea that abstraction could have something as banal as "opinions." Finally, the sentence is completed. "You . . . / . . . Are an epistemological snapshot of the processes / That first mentioned your name at some crowded cocktail / Party long ago . . ." This makes a return to the story, with the same tonal shift as previously noted, the personification of "processes," though without the same wit.

Now we can see chameleon Ashbery in his true colors. "I want that information very much today, / Can't have it, and this makes me angry." Did he not have that information once? No . . . but "someone" did, yet the speaker seems to know that person's billfold and its misadventures very well. He is angry to be denied that information, but who believes he has been denied? What of the story? The story is irrelevant to Ashbery's anger, and because it is, his anger is unbelievable. The story has been abandoned. In its place, Ashbery constructs his metaphorical bridge or poem, "on which people may dance for the feeling / Of dancing on a bridge." If anything attests to Ashbery' superficiality, this begging of the question, this silly tautology does. The surreal image of the speaker seeing his face in the worn stone of the bridge is so transparently solipsistic, who cares? Apparent Ashbery doesn't. The last two lines are worthy of Polonius

and deserve the curtain they hide behind and the sword that runs
them through.

Robert Hass's "Meditation at Lagunitas" is another story, but a
similar one, too. It is another story because its champion at the sym-
posium, Stanley Plumly, is himself a poet whose sympathy for his
subject is more profound than Bloom's for his. Nevertheless,
Plumly's basic assumption about the poem is incorrect. too.

> If this poem is successful it is successful because it moves con-
> vincingly from the easy wit of thinking about loss to a condition
> of fullness, tenderness, from the melancholy of the word to a be-
> lief in the body, from blackberry as a sign to blackberry as
> speech.

To the contrary, this is not why the poem is successful, but why it
fails.

Meditation at Lagunitas

All the new thinking is about loss.
In this it resembles all the old thinking.
The idea, for example, that each particular erases
the luminous clarity of a general idea. The clown-
faced woodpecker probing the dead sculpted trunk
of the black birch is, by his presence,
some tragic falling off from a first world
of undivided light. Or the other notion that,
because there is in this world no one thing
to which the bramble of *blackberry* corresponds,
a word is elegy to what it signifies.
We talked about it late last night and in the voice
of my friend, there was a thin wire of grief, a tone
almost querulous. After a while I understood that,
talking this way, everything dissolves: *justice,*
pine, hair, woman, you and *I.* There was a woman

I made love to and I remembered how, holding
her small shoulders in my hands sometimes,
I felt a violent wonder at her presence
like a thirst for salt, for my childhood river
with its island willows, silly music from the pleasure boat,
muddy places where we caught the little orange-silver fish
called *pumpkinseed*. It hardly had to do with her.
Longing, we say, because desire is full
of endless distances. I must have been the same to her.
But I remember so much, the way her hands dismantled bread,
the thing her father said that hurt her, what
she dreamed. There are moments when the body is as numinous
as words, days that are the good flesh continuing.
Such tenderness, those afternoon and evenings,
saying *blackberry, blackberry, blackberry.*

This poem deflects attention from character development by first
abandoning the friend, mentioned in line 13, and then never fleshing
out the relationship between the speaker and the woman introduced
later. Instead, what we get is an incomprehensible relationship be-
tween the speaker and *blackberries*. Here is the crux of the poem's ap-
peal to the reader: those blackberries signify that language is the real
subject of the poem. The "tragic falling off from the first world / of
undivided light" is that words can never equal things. However,
Adam named the animals in a world before the fall; but really this
is a tedious debate. What we are talking about, as in Ashbery's
poem, is a poet who thinks he has a story to tell, but doesn't believe
it. "It hardly had to do with her," he says, and later adds, "I must
have been the same to her," and we wonder, "Then why are you writ-
ing the poem?" It is apparently an excuse to talk about words in a
fashionable way.

"All the new thinking is about loss. / In this it resembles all the
old thinking." The covered wagons have been drawn into a ring and
the Indians are bearing down on them—the only safety is in beg-

ging the question! Marianne Moore's final revision of her poem "Poetry" included only the first two lines—would that Hass had done the same here. After line two, he has attenuated his intellect as far as it will stretch. He has indeed discovered or articulated a common truth, but he goes on meditating, trying to fill this with examples, like a freshman composition.

The first example, an echo of the first two lines, is that one idea may eradicate another. Hass's notion is old hat—generalities and particulars don't mix. But particulars make a poem: they root us, they capture our attention. So, we get: "the clown-faced woodpecker" and a few lines later the blackberry. But the poet cannot resist summing up what he has already said: "a word is elegy to what it signifies." Why isn't this the first line of the poem? Are poems marshes in which the poet flounders around for good lines? Evidently, to Robert Hass, they are. The line is not first because it risks an emotional impact which the poet believes he is incapable of sustaining.

"We talked about it late last night . . ." introduces a story which the poet soon tires of. He finds his friend boring. So the poet pays lipservice to ideas he would like to use in his story: justice, pine, hair, woman, you and I. This conveniently transports him to *woman*, the one "I made love to and I remembered how, holding / her small shoulders in my hands sometimes, / I felt a violent wonder at her presence." What was he doing to her? Shaking her? Was she radioactive? No, he wants to introduce his childhood. And, of course, that hardly had to do with her. And that's the problem. "Longing, we say, because desire is full / of endless distances." What does that mean? Longing, desire, full, endless, distances, these are words he could have italicized, too. They have about as much meaning as his previous list. They call attention to the breakdown in his thinking. Now he resorts to sentimentality, asking the reader to forgive this collapse. "But I remembered so much, the way her hands dismantled bread, / the thing her father said that hurt her, what she / dreamed." And in that gesture is the inaccuracy that goes hand in hand with it. *Dismantled* bread? And what her father said and what she dreamed—how commonplace can a poem get?

It can get this commonplace: the loose ends must be tied up. "There are moments when the body is as numinous / as words, days that are the good flesh continuing." Hass would like us to nod again and again over the first phrase, one of those arrogant generalizations of contemporary poetry which cannot be debated. But we nod ourselves asleep over the rhetorical second half, a rhetoric Verlaine wished to see strangled. He was right, and this sort of writing, "the good flesh continuing," is typical of the worst of mannered American poetry. Who, as Pound insisted, would ever say that is the pitch of emotion? It was carefully thought out to conform tonally with fashion. Finally, Hass collapses into a sentimental heap. What happened to the poem of the woman, the one he should have written? It gets a nod, "Such tenderness, those afternoons and evenings," but what is important to Hass is this: "The word is elegy to what it signifies"—"*blackberry, blackberry, blackberry.*" Who can take delight in a love poem that ends in intellectual exhaustion?

But what else should we expect? "Meditation at Lagunitas" like "Wet Casements" is a poem about poetry. Either such poems exhaust their own aesthetics or critics do so for them. If their own form is a trope, as John Hollander says, then all the better for the critic.

The Reaper insists that this will not do.

Poetry must be written that casts a cold eye on criticism. Such poetry is being written, but is not discussed at symposiums like After the Flood.

The reason critics write criticism must be understood: they cannot write poems. And, too often today, the poet-critic is more critic than poet.

Look at the way critics talk about poems. Rarely is it illuminating. More and more, it seems to be the jargon of a secret society whose own members, it is highly possible, do not understand each other.

Are poems extolled by critics like Harold Bloom, Richard

Howard, Stanley Plumly, et al, good poems, or merely grist for critical mills? If the latter is true, then they cannot be good poems.

Poetry and criticism are two different things. It is time to remember that the poem comes first.

Wallace Stevens, What's He Done?
Meditation and the Narrative

Roar 'em, whore 'em, cockalorum,
The Muses, they must all adore him,
Wallace Stevens—are we for him?
Brother, he's our father!

Theodore Roethke

To say that Wallace Stevens is the most important influence on contemporary poetry is to say nothing new. However, *The Reaper* is concerned: Is the influence of Wallace Stevens taken for granted? Have his original modes of writing a poem become everyone's modes, so that we have forgotten why we are using them? His line, his imagery, his meditative approach—have all of these been thoroughly assimilated? Is there no reason to question? If so, then *The Reaper* is most concerned.

Wallace Stevens is a wonderful poet. He gives us a program for overcoming the monotony of traditional meters. He demonstrates that it is possible to echo the blank verse line, without being enslaved by it. This goes hand in hand with his treatment of subject. Meditation. When the line is not developing action, it can relax. When the poem does not have to move in a line from A to B, it can meander, with large mannered motions of the poet's mythy mind. This allows the contemporary poet to assume that the dimensions of his thinking are congruent with the dimensions of his subject. After the classical influence of Pound and Eliot, it has been healthy for American poetry to turn in this direction, to ease out of the binding rules set by Pound, to turn away from the examples set by Eliot.

The World as Meditation

> J'ai passé trop de temps a travailler mon violon, à voyager. Mais l'exercice essential du compositeur—la méditation—rien ne l'a jamais suspendu en moi. . .Je vis un rêve permanent, qui ne s'arrête ni nuit ni jour.
> Georges Enesco

Is it Ulysses that approaches from the east,
The interminable adventurer? The trees are mended.
That winter is washed away. Someone is moving

On the horizon and lifting himself up above it.
A form of fire approaches the cretonnes of Penelope,
Whose mere savage presence awakens the world in which
    she dwells.

She has composed, so long, a self with which to welcome
    him,
Companion to his self for her, which she imagined,
Two in a deep-founded sheltering, friend and dear friend.

The trees had been mended, as an essential exercise
In an inhuman meditation, larger than her own.
No winds like dogs watched over her at night.

She wanted nothing he could not bring her by coming alone.
She wanted no fetchings. His arms would be her necklace
And her belt, the final fortune of their desire.

But was it Ulysses? Or was it only the warmth of the sun
On her pillow? The thought kept beating in her like her
    heart.
The two kept beating together. It was only day.

It was Ulysses and it was not. Yet they had met,
Friend and dear friend and a planet's encouragement.
The barbarous strength within her would never fail.

She would talk a little to herself as she combed her hair,
Repeating his name with its patient syllables,
Never forgetting him that kept coming constantly so near.

This late poem by Stevens, from *The Rock*, is like a blueprint of his influence on contemporary poetry. It is full of language that is unsayable as everyday speech, language that exists for the page alone. And yet, at times, it is downright chatty. What an appealing paradox to be able to write in the same poem "The trees had been mended, as an essential exercise / In an inhuman meditation, larger than her own" and "But was it Ulysses? Or was it only the warmth of the sun / On her pillow? The thought kept beating in her like her heart." This like symphonic music: complexly self-referential at one moment and simply melodious at the next. To execute tonal shifts like this in a poem is immensely attractive. And to play off accessible and inaccessible images, one against the other, is attractive, too. "No winds like dogs watched over her at night" is, finally, obscure; whereas "The trees are mended" is profoundly clear as an image of spring. In a poem by Stevens, such inconsistencies breed and thrive.

Consider the subject: The world as meditation and meditation as the waiting of Penelope. In his treatment, Stevens opens more doors than he closes. In other words, he provides more ways for contemporary poets to explore their subjects. If Stevens can succeed with a classical theme, how much easier it is for the contemporary meditating on more personal themes. How does Stevens succeed in this poem? He convinces us that he has some insight into Penelope which is essential to understanding the world: for example, the cycle of the seasons, their leaving and coming back again. She, with her barbarous inner strength, is as much a part of the larger, inhuman meditation of the planet as she is of her own human meditation, which might also be identified as Homer's meditation and, indeed, Wallace Stevens'. Stevens' contemporary counterpart hopes to succeed by convincing us that he has some insight into his *own* life which is essential to understanding *our* world.

Stevens' individuality is breathtaking. Ultimately, of all the moderns, his poems alone are about thinking. Compared to the political ramifications of Pound's poetry and the religious concerns of Eliot's, a poetry free from any context outside itself, which poetry about thinking necessarily is, is enormously liberating. It frees the imagination to impose its own order on the world. In writing about a poem by Marianne Moore, a kindred spirit, Stevens had this to say: "Considering the great purposes that poetry must serve, the interest of the poem is not in its meaning but in this, that it illustrates the achieving of an individual reality." In "The World as Meditation" the reality is not Homer's, nor is it Penelope's, nor is it ours. It is Stevens' alone. But the achievement is breathtaking because he convinces us it is all four.

How does Stevens manage this? To begin with, he makes use of his reading in a pragmatic way—to make poems. The reader is told just enough to understand the source that Stevens is starting from. Everything else is filled in by the poet's imagination. Take, for example, Penelope's passive ordeal. This is Homer's reality. "The World as Meditation" is, first, an assertion that Stevens has assimilated and understood that reality. But "She wanted nothing he could not bring her by coming alone./She wanted no fetchings" and "She would talk a little to herself as she combed her hair" are pure speculation. It is Stevens shading the myth with the pigments of his own imaginings. With regard to this characteristic *The Reaper* thinks of Norman Dubie. He and the other contemporary offspring have been seduced by this manipulation of identifiable realities.

It was not John Berryman who showed us that language could be distorted, so that it could exist only on the page, but Stevens. Taking his cue from Mallarmé, he flies in the face of the Romantic and Modern traditions which require a poet to be a man speaking to men, a man putting words on the page that he might speak out loud in the pitch of emotion. Instead, the verbal complexity of a Stevens poem confines it to the page. The attraction of this to the contemporary is the shift of emphasis from having to know how language sounds around him to having to know only the syntax of his own inner voice. This leads to a kind of verbal play that is hard to resist and can be found in poets as widely divergent as Laura Jensen and Jorie Graham, Sandra McPherson and William Matthews. When we enter the refexive modifying clauses in the third stanza of the "The World as Meditation," it isn't long before we are lost. In fact, by the middle of the second line we are made to forget the whole of the poem and enter the fascination of the part. *The Reaper* has said before that in this poem, as in most poems by Stevens, simple and complex language exists side by side. Nothing attracts attention to the language itself more than such contrasts. Yet what happens when, rather than focusing meditation, language itself becomes the object of meditation, the subject of the poem?

In reaction to the deep image, which stood without context or with one so subtly implied it was invisible, who better to turn to than Wallace Stevens and his discursive picture-making. In his *American Poetry Review* article of January/February 1978, Stanley Plumly came close to explaining this reaction:

> The corrective balance the '70's have provided for the influences
> of the '60's is to remind us that the image alone has no voice.

Yet the poets who have learned from Wallace Stevens are not, despite the widespread interest in a poet's voice, really interested in voice, at all; voice needs to be heard, and cannot really exist when the poem works only on the page. It is not the simplicity of speech, or voice, that intrigues these poets, but the complexity of the silent patterns on the page.

This is the sum of what we have inherited from Wallace Stevens. Unfortunately, his gifts have been misunderstood more often than not, resulting in mannered poems that rely on opaque language. *The Reaper* concludes that in the considerable shadow of Stevens such poems embody a formal twinge—something to be relaxed with tweezers. They are symptoms without his grand disease. For example, here is a poem by Ira Sadoff from *Palm Reading in the Winter*.

A Clear Sky

A clear sky threatens this morning
to overtake our thoughtfulness,
forecast by no one and taking most
by surprise. Yet a few of us
will still be children standing over water
disinterested in reflection, willing
to be quieted by the shock of clouds
passing over the schoolyard suddenly.

If all of us could leave the countryside
or at least forget the thick textures
of shadows which tend to be separate, if we
could be absent as we are permanent, then endings

which clear up so little anyway, might
make their point. But the sunshine in the yard
and the diminished wind will offer hope
we don't deserve: that frozen light
cast over children and their satchels.

To begin at the end, the final image, "that frozen light / cast over children and their satchels," as Plumly would say has no voice. And the rest of the poem's discursive imagemaking provides no image. In the first stanza we have a bit of weather and some children in a schoolyard. This is promising enough, yet all that Sadoff accomplishes is a lot of talk which leads to mistakes like the one in the last two lines of the first stanza. Is it necessary to say a *shock* of clouds passes over *suddenly*? What we have is a pseudo-meditation. Nothing is thought of here. No insight is gained or offered. Hence the conclusion with the voiceless image and, overall, a cardboard Stevens meditation. This should not be, since Sadoff himself, in the middle of the poem, is looking so earnestly for meaning. The complex conditional sentence beginning "If all of us could leave the countryside" should point to the meaning of the poem. But does Sadoff think that "endings, which clear up so little anyway, might make their point" is wisdom? Insight? *The Reaper* would like to know what *is* the point? Looking to what little narrative is here, the children regarding the changing weather, we can find no evidence of a point. It all seems to be summed up in that last image preceded by its ominous colon. The meaninglessness here is doubletalk. And smug doubletalk at that.

That is one problem with Stevens' influence—that a poet can think on paper, make a poem of that thought process, call it a meditation, and still get nowhere. A further problem is that in doing this, he will indulge in distortions of language that serve to obscure his poem even more.

Here is a recent poem by Louise Glück.

World Breaking Apart

> I look out over the sterile snow.
> Under the white birch tree, a wheelbarrow.
> The fence behind it mended. On the picnic table,
> mounded snow, like the inverted contents of a bowl
> whose dome the wind shapes. The wind,
> with its impulse to build. And under my fingers,
> the square white keys, each stamped
> with its single character. I believed
> a mind's shattering released
> the objects of its scrutiny: trees, blue plums in a bowl,
> a man reaching for his wife's hand

across a slatted table, and quietly covering it,
as though his will enclosed it in that gesture.
I saw them come apart, the glazed clay begin
dividing endlessly, dispersing incoherent particles
that went on shining forever. I dreamed of watching that
the way we watched the stars on summer evenings,
my hand on your chest, the wine
holding the chill of the river. There is no such light.
And pain, the free hand, changes almost nothing.
Like the winter wind, it leaves
settled forms in the snow. Known, identifiable—
except there are no uses for them.

    Distortions we find in Stevens, as *The Reaper* has said, make us pause, as Stevens intended, to meditate on the working of the language itself. In this poem by Glück, on the other hand, where statements become complex, language is distorted, and accuracy is in doubt, we are expected to move quickly on. First, there is the question of "the wind / with its impulse to build," when it appears to be in the act of eroding or destroying; if anything, the irony inheres in that the wind *is* creating or shaping, but building is not correct. It is the poet who is building, in fact, and with the alacrity characteristic of this sort of poem, we are shown her at her typewriter, building the poem. Then comes the next piece of distorted language: "I believed / the mind's shattering released / the objects of its scrutiny." This is followed by the mandatory list, evidently to make that statement comprehensible with examples, but also to deflect our attention from its obscurity, and the impossibility of hearing it as speech. Confined, in its opaque wrapper on the page, it seems to cloak a fairly banal idea, anyway: that by perceiving them, we impose order on our surroundings. Unfortunately, this is the heart of the poem. There are some stories which are incidental and used as examples: the backyard in the snow, the man and his wife, and the poet and her lover. But the poet's concern is for the way things come apart. All right. They come apart the way ceramic glaze crackles: "dividing

endlessly, dispersing incoherent particles / that went on shining for-
ever." But is this a description of that process? The word *dividing* im-
plies that, but the rest appears to describe something much more
violent: shattering. Again, we are expected to skim over this inaccu-
racy. *The Reaper* expects something else.

This is a very literary poem, and not just because it is about writ-
ing poetry. It contains homages to Frost (the birch, the mended
fence), Williams (the wheelbarrow and later the bowl of plums),
and, with its mind of winter, Stevens himself. It also seems to be a
response to other contemporary poems; "Meditation at Lagunitas"
by Robert Hass and "The Way Things Work" by Jorie Graham both
come to mind. As a *roman á clef*, then, this poem works; as a medita-
tion it does not, because it says that nothing's working here: "except
there are no uses for them." This is a lie. The "settled forms" she
speaks of have been used to make the poem.

In "The World as Meditation," Stevens extends the known
fiction or tale to include his own imagination, thereby implying that
nothing, not even the settled form, is free from the poet's manipu-
lation. Yet Stevens' approach is through the hint, the shading, the
slight adjustment; Norman Dubie goes about it whole hog. Here is
"For Osip Mandelstam" from *The Illustrations*.

> Almost a century ago eleven mousetraps
> Were set out in large houses in Prague,
> Until now the mice, these iron traps and
> The houses have been ignored, yet tonight
> My wife asleep will hear the unlocking,
> The sentimentality of some necks breaking, and
> Will see eleven old women climbing stairs,
> With dustpans, their stockings
> Falling down, reaching the forgotten
> Traps to sweep them clean of everything
> That was alive in her memory
> And, until now, just inside the walls.
>
> And I hate every last one of you

Who reads this silently or aloud
For being in the next apartment
With your ears against our wall.
You heard her weeping?
You think her breasts are like marble with
A large blue vein standing out? You were
Our friends, and in the yellow evenings
She walks through your rooms
Watering your blank flowers for you.

Your scratching is now
The noise of something just inside the walls.

Though Dubie deflects us from the story of Osip Mandelstam, by saying through his title that the poem is *for* the Russian poet and not *about* him, there are many allusions—some right at the beginning—that suggest the contrary. Prague, though not in Russia, is still an eastern European city. And "iron traps," perhaps the most subtle invention in the poem, suggests Stalinist oppression. "The sentimentality of some necks breaking" is an odd but rather clear image of the consequences of life in a totalitarian society. Even the old women armed with dustpans climbing stairs, their stockings falling down, are included here to make us think more of the work-weary peasant compatriots of Mandelstam than of anyone we know. Dubie adheres to his title by injecting his wife into the poem. In fact, it is she who hears the women climbing the stairs to clean out the mousetraps. Those women are manipulated to the point where they become the poet's agents who sterilize his wife's memory, which exists "just inside the walls." This phrase, repeated in the last line of the poem, is another obvious symbol of imprisonment that can apply to the story of Mandelstam as well as the story of Dubie's marriage. If the reader has any doubt the poet drops all pretense with the lines "And I hate every last one of you / Who reads this silently or aloud / For being in the next apartment / With your ears against our wall." This is the ultimate, mannered, sentimental gesture. The reader has been duped. The entire first stanza is a lure which snares us, which makes us pay attention to and endure the insult. The reader is compared to Stalin's spies. This is unendurable, but if it can be ignored—and any intelligent reader would have to ignore it—we are still left to meditate on why Dubie chose to say it in the first place. Why does he say it? Not because the reader is stupid, but to reinforce the connection between himself and Osip Mandelstam. Through implication he appropriates Mandelstam's story, manipulating it as Stevens does the story of Ulysses and Penelope. Yet, where Stevens is faithful to fine points, Dubie obliterates these because, finally, he is more interested in himself. Stevens would never have let the personal run away with him like this.

We have just examined three instances where the influence of Stevens appears harmful: the meditative aspect, the choice of language, and the narrative. When all three aspects run away with a writer we get a poem like "Sunrise" by Robert Hass.

> Ah, love, this is fear. This is fear and syllables
> and the beginnings of beauty. We have walked the city,
> a flayed animal signifying death, a hybrid god
> who sings in the desolation of filth and money
> a song the heart is heavy to receive. We mourn
> otherwise. Otherwise the ranked monochromes,
> the death-teeth of that horizon, survive us
> as we survive pleasure. What a small hope.
> What a fierce small privacy of consolation.
> What a dazzle of petals for the poor meat.
> Blind, with eyes like stars, like astral flowers,
> from the purblind mating sickness of the beasts
> we rise, trout-shaken, in the gaping air,
> in terror, the scarlet sun-flash
> leaping from the pond's imagination
> of a deadly sea. Fish, mole,
> we are the small stunned creatures

inside these human resurrections, the nights
the city praises and defiles. It's all grandeur
and loss from there. From there we all
walk slowly to the sea gathering scales
from the cowled whisper of the waves,
the menstrual polyphony. Small stars
and blind the hunger under sun,
we turn to each other and turn to each other
in the mother air of what we want.
That is why blind Orpheus praises love
and why love gouges out our eyes
and why all lovers smell their way to Dover.
That is why innocence has so much to account for,
why Venus appears least saintly in the attitudes of shame.
This is lost children and the deep sweetness of the pulp,
a blue thrumming at the formed bone, river,
flame quicksilver. It is not the fire
we hunger for and not the ash. It is the still hour,
one deer come slowly to the stream at dusk,
the table set for abstinence, windows
full of flowers like summer in the provinces
vanishing when the moon's half-face pallor
rises on the dark flax line of hills.

The Reaper throws up its scythe in disgust at this. Would it could throw up Hass's head, or at least dissect it, in order to figure out what he is saying. What is clear is, a legacy from Stevens has been perverted almost beyond recognition. The poem signifies an ultimate retreat from clarity. Who can make sense of

> Fish, mole,
> we are the small stunned creatures
> inside these human resurrections, the nights
> the city praises and defiles. It's all grandeur
> and loss from there.

There is the tonal shift of Stevens, but executed as crudely as fingerpainting by strobe light. Indeed, this seems to be what the poem is all about, but of course that isn't enough. We must lapse into a series of literary allusions, piled one on top of the other, like a Dagwood sandwich.

> That is why blind Orpheus praises love
> and why love gouges out our eyes
> and why all lovers smell their way to Dover.
> That is why innocence has so much to account for,
> why Venus appears least saintly in the attitudes of shame.

Does Hass have only one button to his coat? Do all these literary folk have that much in common? Perhaps Orpheus was metaphorically blinded by love, but was Oedipus or Gloucester? Was Matthew Arnold? And it does not take a blind man to see that Venus, in the attitudes of shame, would very definitely appear least saintly, as would anyone. Hass is babbling. Even when apparently he gets to the point, at the end of the poem, his babble is of the most sentimental sort: the beauty of loneliness.

> It is not the fire
> we hunger for and not the ash. It is the still hour,
> one deer come slowly to the stream at dusk,
> the table set for abstinence, windows
> full of flowers like summer in the provinces
> vanishing when the moon's half-face pallor
> rises on the dark flax line of hills.

And don't be mistaken. He is not talking about solitude or stillness, but abstinence from others—the final withdrawal, a strategy, taken to its furthest, as it has been here, that Wallace Stevens allows for. We are at the mind's end, alone with Robert Hass and his poem, and not with the beautiful palm and fire-fangled bird of Stevens, and God help us!

It is time to say that Stevens' influence has not done much good.

The four poems we have talked about are merely exemplary; they are not exceptions. They are examples that show that the meditative poem, when it departs from a strong narrative, either obvious or implied, meditates only on itself. Somehow, the example of Stevens has allowed this sort of writing.

What must take place is a meditative poetry that is in service to a narrative line. If traditionally the meditation takes as its focus a scene from classical literature or the life of Christ, it is deliberate stupidity not to know that the scene must have a tale to go with it. Though his own monumental intelligence overcame it, Stevens' failing to care more for the tale outside his meditation than for his meditation itself has been passed on to a generation of intellectually inferior offspring. They know what he was doing, but they just can't do it themselves. And who says they must? *The Reaper* detects the ill wind of fashion.

Here is a poem in which meditation occurs as part of narrative, allowing each step of the narration or story its proper weight: "Ice" by Larry Levis.

> Walking home, I see the last ice
> Of winter crusting the yards, and here
> The pale, twisted limbs of a doll left out
> When the children stopped playing, and
> Went indoors, and the first, soft snows
> Came down in the air like stilled speech.
> The houses pass on both sides of me. Each
> With an aunt who is ill, or with a father
> Who has become, at this age, a secret
> Even he cannot know, and who waits to be
> Told what it is, or how its story,
> Without him, can go on. At home,
> I drop a cube of ice into a glass
> Of clear ouzo, and swallow, and see
> Nothing amusing in the way the leaves
> Have held on to their branches all winter,

Or in the way these trees keep standing
For death, in a book about death.
The boy I shot eight ball with last night
In the pool hall told me he'd got syphilis
Again, and from the same woman. When she
Came, sitting on his lap and still dressed
In his car, he said her eyes were almost
Closed, like a hen's at nightfall—the skin
Over them pale and so thin he remembered
Tracing things on paper, as a child.
He laughed, and shrugged it off . . .
I could have told him that the skin
Over the body is fragrant, thin as paper,
And fatal. Instead, I listened only to
The soft click of billiards, and soft curses.
He asked me what I did, and when I told him
He frowned, and said at home his father
Thought most books were bad, and burned
The ones he disagreed with, on the lawn.
We both laughed, though it was colder.
And along the bar now most of the men
Had paid up and gone out with no music
On their lips. Each face, tense with its
Secret, was outliving music, and I knew how
The lights in farmhouses along the river
Would go out quietly and suddenly as they
Arrived. I know how their door sills
Would scrape at a last step—how each of us
Would come alone to the end of a different
Story, and how we would not come back,
Not even in the frosted breath of children
Picking their way home from school, in winter—
And how they would yell to one another, even then,
Never dreaming we could hear their cries.

This story is beautifully and simply symmetrical; none of its symmetry is hidden. The children the speaker mentions in the beginning are again at the end; the boy he shot pool with the night before is not merely a passing ghost; even the boy's own story—of the woman, of his father—is rendered faithfully; the men leaving the bar are not dismissed, or forgotten, but take us with them, creating the poem's strong, moving sense of community. Meditation here does what it must do in any story—make flesh.

Consider the language. Nowhere does it distort the story, because of the author's complete commitment to telling a story. Nowhere is it pointless. Even the shocking image—"he said her eyes were almost / Closed, like a hen's at nightfall"—is not hurled at the reader, but held on to, until it is thoroughly understood. This is the patience of narrative.

But Levis' narrative is obvious. Narrative can be implied, too, as in this poem by Charles Wright.

Dead Color

    I lie for a long time on my left side and my right side
    and eat nothing,
                   but no voice comes on the wind
    and no voice drops from the cloud.
    Between the grey spiders and the orange spiders, no voice
                       comes on the wind . . .

    Later, I sit for a long time by the waters of Har,
    And no face appears on the face of the deep.

    Meanwhile, the heavens assemble their dark map.
    The traffic begins to thin.
    Aphids munch on the sweet meat of the lemon trees.
    The lawn sprinklers rise and fall . . .

    And here's a line of brown ants cleaning a possum's skull.
    And here's another, come from the opposite side.

Over my head, star-pieces dip in their yellow scarves toward
their black desire.

Windows, rapturous windows!

This is a story of the senses, which acknowledges them, in the
end, to be what Blake called them: windows of the soul. The first
line of the poem, an allusion to "The Marriage of Heaven and
Hell," brings with it its own story—that of Ezekiel—and is the
starting point of another story, too—the poem's.

Clearly the poet is meditating on the difference between himself
and Ezekiel or, rather, between his world, without religious re-
demption, and Ezekiel's or Blake's, where such redemption is still
plausible. What they have in common are the senses as windows of
perception; but the difference of what is perceived is the point of
the poem. However, the story of the poem follows a movement
from doubt to conviction, from nothingness to "rapturous win-
dows." Between the two, the poet acknowledges the world's narrative:
the heavens, the traffic, the insects, the gardens, life and death, and
finally the visionary possibilities of all these things, as expressed in
the stars.

Perhaps, Stevens' most negative influence has been to create a
foolish mistrust of the narrative line and its linear simplicity. Of
course, he has had help in this. The point is that the contemporary
reader of poetry looks first for movement merely by association,
making a poet like Levis appear too simple and one like Wright too
difficult.

The Reaper's Non-negotiable Demands

1. Take prosody off the hit list.
2. Stop calling formless writing poetry.
3. Accuracy, at all costs.
4. No emotion without narrative.
5. No more meditating on the meditation.
6. No more poems about poetry.
7. No more irresponsibility of expression.
8. Raze the House of Fashion.
9. Dismantle the Office of Translation.
10. Spring open the Jail of the Self.

1. *Take prosody off the hit list.* To write only with the sentence in mind, to extend it, is to write prose; this is a major defect of contemporary poetry. The sentence is the basic unit of prose, and the line of poetry. Despite the recent interest in prosody, this distinction has more or less disappeared. Too bad. Prosody has become an instrument of accommodation rather than exclusion. It is generally believed that this inclusiveness is healthy, but if everything is poetry then nothing is poetry. Here is an exceptional contemporary poem, by Chase Twichell from her book *Northern Spy.*

Like a Caretaker

> I live here, but do not live here.
> Trash blows through the sky tonight.
> Out of a snowy tree, the stars appear,
>
> drops of ice water, they seem so pure.
> The tree petrifies. They are its parasites.
> I live here, but do not live here.
>
> "Fusion" was the word I loved—its nuclear
> logic. The world with a heart of dynamite.
> Out of a snowy tree, the stars appear
>
> faceted and cold, an elegant prayer
> addressed to death. Death loves black and white.
> I live here, but do not live here.
>
> Creatures are born from atoms, from air
> parentless, and drift like satellites
> out of a snowy tree. The stars appear
>
> to be parts of a machine in disrepair,
> which I do not repair. And for this oversight,
> I live here, but do not live here.
> Out of a snowy tree, the stars appear.

There is much going on here that only someone skilled at prosody could accomplish. Besides mastering the form, a villanelle, Twichell has shown the variety that is the result of a prosodic undercurrent: the traditional caesura in the third line (after the foot) and the surprising one in the first (in the middle of the foot), the coupling of enjambment and rhyme in stanzas three, four, and five, the sight rhyme of "nuclear" and "appear" and its introduction of the new rhymes "prayer," "air," and "disrepair," and even the syllabic balance of the second line of the fifth stanza. The poem is as rich in form as it is in meaning. How is it possible for us to bring these prosodic concerns to the following piece, "Walking," from Gregory Orr's *The Red House?*

Out here in the chill air,
the fabric of each breath
unravels. We walk in tractor
ruts where frozen mud studded
with ice crystals makes,
under our boots, a sound
from my childhood: crunch
of sugar lump in a horse's jaw;
its warm muzzle
works across my palm
which is rigid with a held-back
giggle of fear and pleasure.

Sweetcake, our cat, scoots past
then flops on her side and waits
in a clump of broom-sage
colored the same luminous
orange as her own left haunch.
We laugh to think we love so much
this dumb bundle of fluff.
Back in the cottage, under thick
quilts, our bed's still warm.

Prosodically, there is little going on here besides the use of enjambment. Only one, "a held-back / giggle," works as more than an impulse towards rhythm. Many contemporary poems work this way, and we all know it. Straighten out the enjambments and what do we have? Is it enough to be called poetry? Compared to the poem by Twichell, it looks more like poverty.

2. *Stop call formless writing poetry.* Today's reader is assaulted by a mass of prosaic monotony. All of it sounds the same. There are reasons for this. One is evident in Orr's poem, but a larger reason is

that form itself has been pushed so far, there is no longer anything pushing back. This makes form sound like an autonomous creature who sits down with us to write the poem, relieving the contemporary poet of any responsibility for lax lines, flaccid syntax, and the arbitrary casting of poems into what have been called "ghost forms," e.g. poems in quatrains that are clearly not quatrains, etc. It seems the one requirement a poem must meet is that it move "down the page" compellingly, whether it is unfolding an image or following a narrative. Some poets accomplish this movement quickly, others like to take their time. If the effect is not altogether uniform, due to the greater or lesser loquacity of the poet, then it is certainly predictable. This reduces us to what is tacitly understood: any coupling of words constitutes a form. It takes more than that to constitute the form of a poem. If anything is allowed, then nothing is selective. It is time to remind ourselves that poetry is exclusive. How many contemporary American poets can say like the British formalist Philip Larkin, "Form is nothing to me, content is everything."?

3. *Accuracy, at all costs.* Larkin is a master of form, hence his confidence. Where more often than not a reader will have to grope for a structure where none exists, in Larkin's poems he is released from that task. He seeks and he finds. A master of form, like Larkin, is also freed from the anxiety that breeds inaccuracy. His poetry isn't guesswork; he doesn't say it unless it is so. How many contemporary American poets do the same? Not enough. Here is a poem by Dave Smith that is, unfortunately, representative of the status quo.

Doves Flying

> The blue radiance of one lost dove
> at the edge of first light
> floats in the swooping glint
> of memory, that water swelling
> through each vein of my body.
> I continue to wheel at myself

from the plain composition
of the photograph my child
made among trees, those uncles.
I am no more than I should be.
I am only what I was not
under those winged shadows
before I knew I was
the father you could not keep.
I carry this scene with me
into feedstores and truckstops
manned by boys in numbered
shirts: pines shocked
still on the river's watch,
a darkness I cannot leave
but must enter to find
the small grey house
whose windows slammed
a beating light of confusion
into the eyes of promise.
Far downstream in a field
where vines, like orphans,
rustle for anyone's passage,
I am trying to understand
how the click of a camera
turns to the one door
always bolted and gray.
I take this from my pocket,
having seen you again,
and think of our lives
waiting there, still
under folded wings
as if dreaming themselves,
but not themselves ever again.

The anxiety to scurry down the page here leaves a string of errors in its track. First of all, there are the arbitrary choices yoked by prepositions: "blue radiance of one lost dove," "beating light of confusion" and "eyes of promise." Then, there are the dubious quick sketches in apposition: "memory, that water swelling / through each vein of my body," "trees, those uncles" and "veins, like orphans." Finally, there is that generalized language masquerading as insight with a wash of morality: "I am no more than I should be," "I am only what I was not," "I am trying to understand" and "but not themselves ever again." In all of this, Dave Smith is not alone. Inaccuracy is pandemic; the above examples are merely symptoms. However, there are pockets of health. Here is a poem by Vern Rutsala.

Northwest Passage

Out past Sylvan Beach is the place
They still call Indian Village
Built only to be burned
The summer Spencer Tracy came to town

For years after that
Whole families would picnic there
Scavenging the debris
For rubber arrowheads

But when Spencer came
Everyone got jobs
Five dollars a day and lunch
The Depression ending with glamour

And the chance to sew on a button
For a star
Some of the men were extras
Growing beards and wearing buckskin

Rogers' Rangers looking for that passage
All summer long
From eight to five
My father was among them

And once years later
The summer after he died
I saw the movie on the late show
I stared at it hard

Even recognized a few landmarks
I scavenged every frame
For the smallest sign of him
I found none

The quatrains are episodic, and accuracy itself is the point. There are "rubber arrowheads," and there is, finally, no sentimental trace of the father.

4. *No emotion without narrative.* Emotion is inconsequential unless it is the result of a story. The story is communal; it is for others. The inconsequential emotion is the one felt only by the poet himself. In Smith's poem, we have his insular meditation on a photograph—of himself. Rutsala's emotion is just as personal as Smith's but we are granted access to it through narrative.

5. *No more meditating on the meditation. Reaper* readers will recognize a favorite theme here. That the act of writing itself, as a metaphor for thinking, is an adequate subject is a lie. In such a poem the author has lost touch with the world; the associations he makes make sense only to himself and appear random to others. How do you avoid writing such poetry? Look outward and not inward, know others not thyself, give the story not the gloss, find a subject.

6. *No more poems about poetry.* We mean NO MORE POEMS ABOUT POETRY.

7. *No more irresponsibility of expression.* If you have a subject you must be faithful to it; if you are faithful, then you have a responsibility—to express the subject faithfully. By the same token, if you have a form, then you have limits. Pushing a poem to its limits means pushing it no farther. Obviously, *The Reaper* does not clamor for a return to the heyday of rhyme and meter, the elegant formal poem, but for a preoccupation with prosody, even in free verse, that will require the new poet to be a master of phrasing, of lines, of stanzas, of form itself. In other words, anything he says must fit. In the following poem by James Galvin, from his book *Imaginary Timber*, we find just what we are talking about: a free verse poem with an implicit acknowledgement of its own limits, of its lines and stanzas; its rhythm is what rhythm should be—an accumulation of correct line endings and accents in the line falling where they are meant to without being forced. Most importantly, the subject is welded to the form.

Navigation

Evergreens have reasons
For stopping where they do,
At timberline or the clean edge
Of sage and prairie grass.
There are quantities of wind
They know they cannot cross.
They come down from the tundra
On waves of ridges and stop,
Staring out over open country,
Like pilgrims on the shore
Of an unexpected ocean.
The sky is still the sky, they know;
It won't understand ordinary language.

Meet my mother, twice removed,
Who could tell the time from stars.

She said everything is its own reward,
Grief, poverty, the last word.
Evening was her favorite time
And she walked along the shore of trees,
Carrying herself as if afraid
She might give herself away.
She called this being quiet.

Just inside the treeline, out of the wind,
Father built a handrail along the path.
She'd stand there like a sailor's wife
And stare at the high plains as dark came on.
She said mountains might be islands
But the sky is still the sky.
She'd wait for the ranch lights
On the prairie to come out
Like a fallen constellation.
She said waiting is its own reward,
The lights are only reasons.

8. *Raze the House of Fashion.* Writers will always be building this house and it will always be necessary to tear it down. Whoever inhabits it at the moment, surrealists or mannerists, meditative poets or narrative poets, as soon as the crowd begins flocking to its door, it's time to go the other way and, if you're inclined, get your bulldozer.

9. *Dismantle the Office of Translation.* American life tends to be a leveller; things are graded down to mediocrity. In translation into American, great poets from other languages become indistinct from one another. Although as translator a poet like Merwin or Bly might lend a distinctive note, are we to believe Neruda sounds like Merwin or that Transtrommer sounds like Bly? Are we to believe that Rilke sounds like his corporation of translators? In our haste to make the globe smaller, we have lost sight of individuality. Certainly, translation itself is not the problem, but the American mass production

and marketing of it is. The common complaint that poets are reduced in translation should be accompanied by another complaint that in the atmosphere of reverence surrounding them, too much of their bad work gets translated, too. What else could account for the alarming badness of most translations no matter whom they are of? And what is the recent fascination for poets like Seamus Heaney and Geoffrey Hill, an Irishman and an Englishman, if it is not a longing for the sound of a native speech? English.

10. *Spring open the Jail of the Self.* The self will always be with us, but it is not all that we have. Philip Larkin's generation believed that a poet must imagine a distinctive self; he has done so, and it is evident in the following poem, from his latest book, *High Windows*. But there is much more here, too.

Sad Steps

Groping back to bed after a piss
I part thick curtains, and am startled by
The rapid clouds, the moon's cleanliness.

Four o'clock: wedged-shadowed gardens lie
Under a cavernous, a wind-picked sky.
There's something laughable about this,

The way the moon dashes through clouds that blow
Loosely as cannon-smoke to stand apart
(Stone-coloured light sharpening the roofs below)

High and preposterous and separate—
Lozenge of love! Medallion of art!
O wolves of memory! Immensements! No,

One shivers slightly, looking up there.
The hardness and the brightness and the plain
Far-reaching singleness of that wide stare

Is a reminder of the strength and pain
Of being young; that it can't come again
But is for others undiminished somewhere.

The self is a jail, but the world is not. In "Sad Steps" Larkin knows his place in the world. That is the key to unlocking the jail of self: know your place in the world, for God's sake.

The Elephant Man of Poetry

What does *The Reaper* mean by a poetry with a narrative focus? First, it is clear that the term "narrative" is not specific enough. A poem may describe the milkman making his rounds through the neighborhood; he comes home to his wife in bed with the postman. A case can be built (and is in many quarters) for this as "narrative," and after a journalistic fashion it is. Yet it lacks the elements of true storytelling that enable writers like Homer and the Brothers Grimm to endure. What these and other writers discovered is that a story begins with need. The poet must make sense of a situation that is troubling him and say it to someone else; the reader needs to make sense of the world, which troubles us all. The story of the milkman will not help us anymore than the evening news. But the poet who beguiles the reader with the story itself will answer that need in all of us—to learn about and understand our lives. Only when the story as a whole becomes a metaphor does this understanding occur. The poet's responsibility is not to meditate on his process of devising a story; it is to tell the story as if he were discovering it line by line. This process will fulfill the need of poet and reader. It will render the experience and its comprehension through the poem memorable.

American poetry has become anecdotal: short narratives con-

cerning interesting or amusing events are sprinkled through medita-
tions. These small stories are objects of the poet's beguilement.
Even the prime example of narrative in our era, *Audubon, A Vision* by
Robert Penn Warren, is a meditation containing a story—part II,
"The Dream He Never Knew the End of." In this segment the pro-
tagonist and an Indian, after spending a winter night in a cabin with
a woman and her two sons, suddenly see them taken and hanged. It
is the longest section of a poem of seven sections, and it is the most
compelling. But it is not the point of the poem. The point is to
meditate on this: "How thin is the membrane between himself
(Audubon) and the world." What purpose then does the story serve?
It is not the whole but a part of the larger meditation. It could stand
outside the context of the larger poem, and it makes Warren's final
statement, "Tell me a story," seem rather to mean *Tell me an anecdote.*
For that is what he has done—told us an anecdote.

Yet the final line of the poem, "Tell me a story of deep delight,"
makes us respond, "Yes, tell us one!" If this is a "century, and mo-
ment of mania" should a story be a flight from that? *Audubon* is, ap-
parently. *The Reaper* says it should not be. Warren's success as a poet
has been to leave his readers hungering for more. In an age of di-
eters we're all supposed to get up from the table hungry for more.
What is it we are hungry for? We are hungry for stories that are not
merely pieces of journalism or anecdotes. Warren knows this, but
do we see it in the fraudulent history and persona poems being
turned out at present? The problem is one of comprehension. The
poet must comprehend that the story is more important than his
observations about it, and that the story must comprehend the
poem. The story **is** the poem. The poet does this for the reader, not
for himself. If he is successful the stories themselves, their plots, be-
come objects of beguilement for the reader. Consider these plots.

Two people return to visit the ruins of a small town and farm.
One of them, a guide, shows his companion a brook that runs by a
place where a house used to stand. In the brook is a cup he stole
from a children's playhouse. As a symbolic act, he offers his com-

panion a drink from the cup, assuring him that the water has a magical power of restoring order out of chaos. The guide is the narrator of the poem. The companion is the reader.

An overworked woman near physical and mental exhaustion, whose husband is a failure, engages some campers beside a lake in the story of her life. She is haunted by the madness of her uncle who, before she was born, was caged upstairs in her father's house. She imagines her parents' marriage, especially her mother, in that situation and mentions that she, too, has been caged—but in the state asylum. She is wasting time by telling her story, but it is time she needs to waste.

A successful professor, who visits his home town occasionally, must spend the night on one of these visits sharing a hotel room with a man he doesn't trust. His roommate, a robust, magnanimous collector for a local paper, detects this mistrust immediately and attempts to bridge the gap by offering the frightened professor the collars he has outgrown. A disarming absurdity. The collector has not lost touch with his region as the professor has. The absurdity of his offer is tempered by his forthright manner in describing his occupation and the professor's fear.

After years of telling one another a lie, a mother and her son tell a stranger who is staying the night the truth. Years before, her dead husband killed a man who was her lover. Afterward, the two of them buried the corpse in the cellar. One night, when her son was still a baby, the skeleton arose from the grave. The woman, with the help of her husband (who could not see or hear it), trapped the skeleton in the attic and nailed the door shut. The family lie, expressed by the son, is that they did not know the man. The mother and son, two old believers, live in a world of the dead.

An old fat woman, ensconced in her kitchen, tells a visitor that her daughter has left her common law husband and married another man. The jilted man is a bad farmer, and the mother and daughter moved in with him and subsequently supported him. His one obsession, almost an artistic one, is for his chickens. The old woman describes his passion lovingly, but her sympathies, despite the visitor's protestations, are finally with her daughter. When the poor farmer, having heard the news, returns and unburdens himself to the visitor, the old woman, getting in the last word, rejects him, too.

A couple, returning late at night to their remote farm, pause outside the barn when the woman is sure she has seen a man's face by the lantern light. By their conversation they imply that this is not just any stranger. In fact, it is someone they both know—the wife, especially. She believes the man has come for something, possibly for her. When it turns out that it is only a father and his child taking a long after-bedtime walk the woman, relieved, turns to her husband and finds him gone. She drops her lantern and is left alone in the dark.

A young couple on a commonplace excursion through the countryside come upon a uncommon thing: a brook whose waters run counter to all the other brooks in the region. The woman sees it as a symbol of their intimacy and names it, almost as if it were their child. The man, at first pragmatic, at her urging becomes prophetic and rhetorical, meditating aloud on the brook as an emblem of existence. It is the woman who brings him back to earth again, and the poem is the story of their marriage.

A man in a small town, having failed at hard scrabble farming, burns his ancient farmhouse down and with the fire insurance buys a telescope. No one in this little society is fooled by what he has done, but they accommodate it as they accommodate their thieves who, if they can, return what they have stolen. After all, as the narrator implies, what the man has done has an enduring necessity about it. He and his telescope become a link between that isolated community and the universe.

You cannot find stories like these today in American poetry. You might even be hard pressed to find them in contemporary fiction. Summarized here, these plots are still fresh and riveting. They are all plots discovered by Robert Frost in his poems. Now don't turn the channel. Keep your hand away from that dial. *The Reaper* said Robert Frost. You may have recognized these plots and even know the poems, and certainly as summaries they do not replace the poems. What they show is the wholeness of the poems as stories.

There is an anecdote that has Robert Frost and Wallace Stevens trading insults. Supposedly Stevens said to Frost, "The trouble with you, Robert, is that you write about subjects." Frost retorted, "The trouble with you, Wallace, is that you write bric-à-brac." What critic has better summed up the work of these poets then they themselves? Regardless of their opinions of one another, today's fashion clearly favors bric-à-brac. This does not satisfy our need for good stories *in poetry*. Robert Frost, of all his contemporaries is the poet who can show us how to tell them. *The Reaper* finds it amazing and appalling that, apparently, few want to learn.

What is it about Frost that is so offputting? Randall Jarrell in his essays "The Other Frost" and "To the Laodiceans" showed the difference between the Public Frost and what he actually wrote. Still, Jarrell praised much more of Frost than is actually praiseworthy. All the same, anyone who takes exception to Frost because his narrative poems are in blank verse is not worth arguing with. That reader may now leave this essay. Frost has something to teach. Let's return to the poems.

What are the aspects of these poems' narrative structures? *Narration, character, setting, exposition, dialogue, conflict, climax, dénouement*—the elements of fiction. Since each of the poems we have summarized contain these elements, more or less, *The Reaper* intends to focus on the manipulation of one element in each poem. If you want to learn a new bag of tricks, pull some important rabbits out of your hat, change water to wine, lead into gold, your enemies into animals, and your friends into bodies of water, follow *The Reaper*.

The title of "Directive" immediately puts the reader in touch with the narrator, for it is he who guides the reader, his companion, back to the beginning of the story. What is fascinating about the poem is that to do this the narrator must begin at the end.

> Back out of all this now too much for us,
> Back in a time made simple by the loss
> Of detail . . .

Simple enough. Frost's narrator remains just that, a narrator. He takes us step by step of the way, whether it is backwards or forwards. The integrity of the story is never violated by unwarranted side-trips. In "Directive" we are going back in time; our destination is the source of the story.

> Make yourself up a cheering song of how
> Someone's road home from work this once was,
> Who may be just ahead of you on foot
> Or creaking with a buggy load of grain.
> The height of the adventure is the height
> Of country where two village cultures faded
> Into each other. Both of them are lost.
> And if you're lost enough to find yourself
> By now, pull in your ladder road behind you
> And put a sign up CLOSED to all but me.

Never has the narrator of a poem been more intimate with his reader, and this does not mean making him privy to dark personal secrets. It means being there with him. On the same journey. In this way, he fulfills his need to tell the story. What of the reader's need to hear it? How is he enticed to listen? The first line includes him—"too much for us"—and then he is promised a past, a place in the story. And that place is identified by the narrator as "your waters and your watering place. / Drink and be whole again beyond confusion." What narrator has ever been more generous? The point is that the narrator of "Directive" introduces a series of confusing details, the detail of ruin,

> There is a house that is no more a house
> Upon a farm that is no more a farm
> And in a town that is no more a town.

Then restores, if not brick and mortar, at least their emotional importance: "This was no playhouse but a house in earnest." From this confusion, the narrator constructs before our eyes, an ordered whole. That is the narrator's job. Frost's narrators succeed at the job time and again because their role is to tell a story; the story is being sought out, for the reader's sake.

"A Servant to Servants" could be called a dramatic monologue, but the character is telling the story of her life. In that telling, the reader discovers one of the most memorable characters in American literature. She is not memorable because she serves the poet's whimsy, but because she convinces the reader she is the only character who could live this tale. How is it so? The most obvious device is the use of colloquial expression.

> I didn't make you know how glad I was
> To have you come and camp here on our land . . .
>
> I can't express my feelings, any more
> Than I can raise my voice or want to lift
> My hand (Oh, I can lift it when I have to).
> Did ever you feel so? I hope you never . . .
>
> I see it's a fair, pretty sheet of water,
> Our Willoughby! How did you hear of it?
> I expect, though, everyone's heard of it.
> In a book about ferns? Listen to that!
>
> He looks on the bright side of everything,
> Including me. He thinks I'll be all right
> With doctoring . . .

To this day, this is what Frost is known for—his use of what he called "sentence sounds" in blank verse. But his ear for the American language is so right here, that it makes little difference how it scans; this is as good as anything in William Carlos Williams. What is exceptional about the whole poem is how character is developed. Here is a character who is mentally disturbed, but not a sordid case history; her frankness about herself startles us. We can imagine the people she is talking to drawing away, but we are drawn to her. Even the anecdote she tells about her father's mad brother, and how when she was first married her mother had to listen in bed to her brother-in-law ranting upstairs in his cage is an emblem of her own distress. She would not be the character she is if the reader felt like a confessor. She has tested the boundaries of her existence and found there is no way out. Her husband's failure, her daily drudgery, the congenital madness, out her window "the fair, pretty sheet of water," these strangers listening to her story, and the pathetic sense that she may endure the unendurable are almost too much to bear. You can hear her saying long before *The Unnameable*, "I can't go on, I'll go on," but more like a flesh and blood character from Tolstoy than Beckett's eloquent phantom. She is a character with a life of her own. Whatever the poet has imparted from his own life is a seamless part of her. She does not need the corroboration of the busy poet as narrator interjecting, "Here's an interesting person I know." When poets do that they are invariably drawing attention to themselves and away from their story. In contemporary poetry, a poet might try to create such a character, but it would be a persona. To call "A Servant to Servants" a persona poem would not be accurate. It is a piece of fiction.

A successful fictional setting in a poem is a fertile confinement. In "A Hundred Collars" the hotel room the two men must share is as close-fitting as a collar. This is reflected in the locations named, Lancaster that "bore" the professor, ironically, "such a little town, such a great man" and Woodsville Junction, where he is stranded for the night, "a place of shrieks and wandering lamps and cars that shock and rattle—and *one* hotel." Even more than the dialogue between the professor and the collector, the setting clarifies the differences between the two—the professor who has lost touch with his region and is at home nowhere, and the collector who is at ease anywhere.

After we leave the hotel lobby, and the night clerk leads the professor "up three flights of stairs / And down a narrow passage full of doors," we come to a small room which is like a stage set—two beds for two men. The size of the collector, already occupying the room, emphasizes its smallness. First, there is the professor's point of view.

> A man? A brute. Naked above the waist,
> He sat there creased and shining in the light.
> Fumbling the buttons in a well-starched shirt.

Then there is the collector's description of himself, an expansive man, growing like a tree.

> "I'm moving into a size-larger shirt.
> I've felt mean lately; mean's no name for it.
> I just found what the matter was tonight:
> I've been a-choking like a nursery tree
> When it outgrows the wire band of its name tag."

He contrasts vividly with the professor who shrinks into his anonymity and hurries to the other bed.

> The Doctor made a subdued dash for it,
> And propped himself at bay against a pillow.

The character is held at bay, or rather holds himself there, for the rest of the poem, cowering in the traditional symbols of surrender. The reader might feel contempt for him, but the collector, magnanimous to the end, offers to remove the professor's shoes. The professor's reaction to this gesture is exactly what the setting demands it should be.

> "Don't touch me, please—I say, don't touch me, please.
> I'll not be put to bed by you, my man."

Here the collector indulges in a little good-natured contempt,

("Who wants to cut your number fourteen throat!"), and then offers, if the professor will do the same, to put his money out in an act of good faith. Finally, the professor is relieved enough to listen to the collector's bedtime story, and that is what he gets. The story, about the collector's job for a regional paper, riding from farm to farm, is sort of an idyll of the New England countryside, and is especially telling and appropriate in that it describes the land the professor has forsaken.

> The fields are stripped to lawn, the garden patches
> Stripped to bare ground, the maple trees
> To whips and poles. There's nobody about.
> The chimney, though, keeps up a good brisk smoking.
> And I lie back and ride.

After his story, like an adult who has tucked a child in bed, the collector departs; he's "just begun the night," but will be back. And the professor, imitating the way the collector rides easily on his horse, slides a little down his pillow. The setting clasps him like a specimen.

There are two types of exposition in "The Witch of Coös." First, the traditional sort that, in effect, brings us to the present, telling us where we are and whom we are with; it occurs in the first three lines of the poem.

> I stayed the night for shelter at a farm
> Behind the mountain, with a mother and son,
> Two old-believers. They did all the talking.

You cannot get more compact than that. The second sort, which is integral to the plot, involves the exposing of a lie. At her son's urging, the mother begins a tall tale, a gesture of friendship toward a stranger. However, although the woman is true to the telling of her tale, the reader becomes aware gradually that falsehood is being peeled away. This happens again and again in Frost's poems: the more we get of the story, the closer we come to the truth. In this case, the tale resolves into a confession of family conflict, which involves exposition, reaching back into the past and exposing its true nature. Exposition is usually a banal necessity of fiction, giving certain information one needs to follow the story. Knowing what we know by the end of the poem, that the skeleton in the attic was a man the woman's husband killed instead of her, the details of the poem's last two lines take on a haunting significance.

> I verified the name next morning: Toffile.
> The rural letter box said Toffile Lajway.

Since the poem is a metaphorical whole, discrete lines in it are illuminated. We can return to what the women said early in the poem

> Don't that make you suspicious
> That there's something the dead are keeping back?
> Yes, there's something the dead are keeping back.

and understand that the living have something to keep back, too.

To write dialogue in any medium requires an ear for speech; to write it as Frost does, constrained by blank verse, is a most rigorous task. But as *The Reaper* has said, the metrics are beside the point. The point is that Frost's people sound genuine. Part of the compression of Frost's poems is that the characters reveal themselves by what they say about themselves and others. All they need is someone to talk to, and in "The Housekeeper," the narrator, "I," offers himself as a sounding board. But he is also more than a sounding board; he is building bridges for her to cross with characters—herself, her daughter, and her son-in-common law.

And the dialogue builds a poem; it's not just talk. It constructs a metaphor for the dissolution of a family, albeit a family of convenience. Solely through dialogue, the reader comes to an understanding of Estelle's leaving John to marry another man, of John's failure as a farmer and obsession with raising chickens, and of the housekeeper's pragmatism. The narrator, who has moral reservations about what Estelle has done, decides he cannot face his friend, but he has been entwined in the old woman's conversation and is caught. At first, he only wants to know the gossip.

> "You've heard? Estelle's run off."
> "Yes, what's it all about? When did she go?"

Then, at the end of the poem, enlightened he wants to escape.

> "Then it's all up. I think I'll get away.
> You'll be expecting John. I pity Estelle;
> I suppose she deserves some pity, too.
> Your ought to have the kitchen to yourself
> To break it to him. You may have the job."

> "You needn't think you're going to get away.
> John's almost here. I've had my eye on someone
> Coming down Ryan's Hill. I thought 'twas him.
> Here he is now."

It is too late. John arrives, and the narrator must perform his duty as a friend and listen again to the story he already knows. The warning implicit in this poem is that if you listen to a story, if you open yourself to it, you may become involved as a character yourself. This is the mastery of Frost's dialogue. The reader saying to himself all the parts of the poem becomes a player, incapable of detachment. This is the point in Shakespeare as well as in Frost.

A conventional treatment of the conflict in "The Fear" would be satisfied with the situation of a couple standing late at night in a remote rural area, frightened by something they cannot see in the darkness. Frost takes us one step further by introducing the conflict between husband and wife. He uses a familiar conflict to illuminate an unfamiliar one. The familiar conflict is this: one person is afraid of the dark, the other is not. In "The Fear" the conflict is complicated by the wife's desire to contact someone she believes is out there and her husband's indifference.

"And I can't stand it. Joel, let me go!"

"But it's nonsense to think he'd care enough."

"You mean you couldn't understand his caring.
Oh, but you see he hadn't had enough—
Joel, I won't—I won't—I promise you.
We mustn't say hard things. You mustn't either."

"I'll be the one, if anybody goes!
But you give him the advantage with this light.
What couldn't he do to us standing here!
And if to see was what he wanted, why,
He has seen all there was to see and gone."

Her cry out to the darkness "What do you want!" breaks her from
Joel, and her fear finally materializes as an unfearful thing—a father
and his child out for a walk. A conventional resolution here would
call for a sigh of relief on the husband's and wife's part, maybe even
a conjugal "I told you so," but that is not what happens. Instead, the
wife insists on her fear to the exclusion of everyone else, so that her
last speech to—the strangers? to Joel?—is ambiguous in its address.

"But if that's all—Joel—you realize—
You won't think anything. You understand?
You understand that we have to be careful.
This is a very, very lonely place.—
Joel!"

Insistent to the end, the woman turns to Joel who has already gone
back into the house. Her lantern drops to the ground and she is left
in darkness to face her fear alone.

She spoke as if she couldn't turn.
The swinging lantern lengthened to the ground,
It touched, it struck, it clattered and went out.

Frost shows us that the poem is an excellent instrument for discovering the complexity of conflict.

Climax in Frost takes may shapes. Each story determines its own. In "West-Running Brook" a young couple discovers what they need from each other. Here their sexual give-and-take is in their speeches about the brook. Hers is intimate, his lofty—both are apt. The climax comes in the synthesis of the two, which is her last word. After his speech she says,

> "Today will be the day
> You said so."

> "No, today will be the day
> You said the brook was called West-Running brook."

> "Today will be the day of what we both said."

In the usual dramatic sense, even in Frost, climax is an explosive fragmentation. Here it is unifying and quiet. Once again, we come to the end and the poem is whole. Out of contraries Frost has found integrity. The definition of wholeness today does not have to do with the poem's wholeness but with the poet's, getting the whole man or woman as poet down on the page. That is, sacrificing the poem for the poet's self-healing labor. No wonder we have so little interest in each other's poems and crave something else.

Frost's concept of wholeness includes untying knots of confusion. How does one act toward a man who has burned his house down and spent the insurance money on something as apparently frivolous as a telescope? In "The Star Splitter" the answer is to embrace him. It is a poem of denouement, the untying of a knot. How does this small society accommodate such a man?

> Out of a house and so out of a farm
> At one stroke (of a match), Brad had to turn
> To earn a living on the Concord railroad,
> As under-ticket-agent at a station

Where his job, when he wasn't selling tickets,
Was setting out, up track and down, not plants
As on a farm, but planets, evening stars
That varied in their hue from red to green.

His eccentricity, implicitly accepted by the society, is made part of
the poem's metaphorical whole, as seen in the passage above. That
is, it is accepted, too, by the poet, and by his emissary, the poem's
narrator.

Bradford and I had out the telescope.
We spread our two legs as we spread its three,
Pointed our thoughts the way we pointed it,
And standing at our leisure till the day broke,
Said some of the best things we ever said.

"Some of the best things we ever said"—that is as telling a line as
you can find anywhere in Frost. It describes the relationship between
the poet and his poems. They are constructed out of the elements
of fiction into poems to enable himself and his characters to say
themselves better than they ever have. Understanding this, the last
six lines of "The Star Splitter," those three questions, seem to ask
if this is not the way it has always been.

We've looked and looked, but after all where are we?
Do we know any better where we are,
And how it stands between the night tonight
And a man with a smoky lantern chimney?
How different from the way it ever stood?

By looking at how these poems work, *The Reaper* acknowledges
Frost's strong suit—the narrative—and insists on his inclusion
among the poets we turn to for guidance and delight. Furthermore,
as an American poet he has no peer. We can learn more about telling
stories in poems from Frost than from any other writer. In an era in

which more and more readers are clearly insisting on stories that encompass us all, it is clear that only the dull witted will persistently avoid Frost in favor of self-analytical bric-à-brac, of fragments instead of the whole. It is time to indict this persistence by recognizing it for what it is. On the part of the reader it is a result of conditioning, of reading fragmented verse until he believes that stories are nothing more than remnants in an ancient bone house. On the part of the poet it is a result of uncertainty with regard to subject. The contemporary poet views his subject through tunnel vision. He knows all sorts of characters and situations lie to either side of him, but he is unwilling—because he is afraid—to include them and deal with them. For this reason, and for trivial ones, such as the formal properties of his poems, this fear is transferred to Robert Frost and indulged by various stupid spokesmen for contemporary poetry and criticism. One can imagine them as young men and women having to live in the shadow of the great man. Now that he's been dead for nearly twenty years, they play on the ugly facts of his life and opinions as a public man and ignore the unparalleled accomplishment of the work itself. Fortunately, the poetry of Ezra Pound has overcome the prejudice against the man. It is time the poetry of Robert Frost did, too.

The Reaper Interviews
Jean Doh and Sean Dough

The Reaper traveled to Jean and Sean's walk-up farmhouse in the city and found them relaxing in the evening after a long day of blurb writing. As Sean made drinks with Puerto Rican white rum, Jean circumambulated the apartment, spraying her Maidenhair ferns with an atomizer. From the kitchen, Sean would call out lines of poetry that had struck him, bolts of inspiration, and Jean would respond, still attentive to her plants, with approving giggles, solemn silences, and an occasional grunt of reservation. A photograph of Jean pouting seductively on the cover of *The American Poetry Review* dominated the wall above the couch where the Reaper sat. In front of the couch, the oriental coffee table was littered with literary journals of all sorts, including the first four issues of *The Reaper* prominently though casually displayed on top of a recent *Antaeus* of Sydney Greenstreet-like proportions. Jo Jo, the pet dog of indeterminate breed, ran back and forth in the long living room where windows alternated with dark, dense banks of books. A pair of Guatemalan breastplates gleamed menacingly over the fireplace, and along the mantelpiece Latin American bric-à-brac abounded. On an end table beside the couch was a photograph of a starving child, Sean and Jean's adopted daughter who lives in Paraguay. A forty-eight inch screen and Betamax machine sat in the center of the room and reminded the Reaper of this literary couple's profound love for the cinema. However, it was later revealed that they had been watching their interview with Bill Moyers. Our own interview began when Sean, dressed in Libyan jelaba, entered from the kitchen to serve us drinks in metal mugs.

The Reaper:	We'd like to thank you for agreeing to this interview with us. We know how busy your schedules are.
Jean:	We're more than happy to help a struggling magazine get off the ground. You know we've found your first four issues to be very entertaining. It seems whenever I get together with my friends one more of them is stinging from a Reaper rebuke. *(Laughter)*
Sean:	*(Laughing)* We've been waiting to be roasted ourselves. *(Laughter)* And now, here you are interviewing us. We guess that's a good sign. *(Long uncomfortable silence)*
The Reaper:	Jean, we'll start with you. Where is the narrative line in your work?
Jean:	I began writing poetry when I was very young, and naturally I was influenced by just about everything I read! I read the Beats, the Black Mountain poets; the Deep Image affected me deeply. I went back to the Surrealists, and I went ahead to the New Formalists.
The Reaper:	But the narrative line?
Jean:	Well, I opened Robert Frost: the poems were so long! And by that time I was publishing a lot myself. I didn't have time to write a narrative line! I hope that answers your question.
The Reaper:	Well, it will have to. Sean, in the last year Jean has

garnered a tidy collection of awards, her poems have appeared in every major literary journal, and when she returned from her diplomatic mission to Tierra del Fuego her picture was on the front page of *The New York Times*. How does that make you feel?

Sean: I'm happy for Jean. I've applauded her successes from the moment we met in graduate school. In fact, it was Jean who turned me to poetry. I was writing fiction, but I was having trouble telling a story. I'll never forget what Jean said: "Hey, you don't have to worry about that in a poem." That changed my life. Suddenly, poems started coming out of nowhere. You know the rest.

The Reaper: Oh? We're not sure . . .

Sean: Oh, you know.

The Reaper: OK. We guess so. Given the fact that Jean first interested you in poetry, she must have been a strong influence. When did you first realize that she was one poet and you were another?

Sean: Turning twenty-one is a tremendous event in all of our lives. Each of us turns twenty-one only once.

The Reaper: It was when you turned twenty-one?

Sean: No, it was *like* turning twenty-one. It was a leaping off point from being responsible to other people to being responsible *for* other people. Now, all of us know that it is very difficult to write poetry in America. It is doubly difficult if you are married to a poet. And it is triply difficult when she is successful and you're not. So when Jean had her breakdown, and solicitations for her work started backing up, some-

	one had to write those poems. I did that. And that's when I realized I just wasn't Jean.
Jean:	Sean was like a brother to me. And a husband, of course. And a best friend.
Sean:	What's the point of writing poems if you don't live like a poet? Besides, I have been enjoying a little notoriety myself, lately.
The Reaper:	Yeah, *The Battle of Borodino: A Book of Haiku.*
Jean:	The inspiration for that was our Russian-Japanese gardener, you know.
Sean:	Yes, old Boris Hayakawa. I was trying to leap out of the self. I had felt that my work for several years was stymied, so I wanted to look at other characters around me. I felt a tremendous urge to expand, to reach out, to embrace a greater reality. One day I was standing out in the yard, supervising Boris. And I thought to myself, "What a quaint character! What a wonderful personality. What must he think while he is cultivating the radishes, while he is trowelling the turnips?" I felt a tremendous sudden empathy. . .
Jean:	Like beating of enormous wings.
Sean:	Exactly. What was his life really like? Did he watch television? Did he read? Did he know that he gardened for famous authors? I wondered if it had any effect on his reality at all. And I found that by thinking about this long enough, by concentrating on Boris, I was able to leap out of the self—
Jean:	To a greater awareness of the self.
Sean:	Yes! What I realized in writing about other people

and their lives was that I was really writing about my *own* life. In other words, the more I wrote about these people, the more I realized that their lives were no more interesting than my own! In fact, their lives didn't mean anything unless I put them into the context of my own life.

Jean: That's the marvelous circular accomplishment of *The Battle of Borodino*. It all comes back to the self.

Sean: Yes, and to *my* self in particular.

The Reaper: Jean, you appear to be in complete agreement with Sean about the self. Your long poem, "Amino Acids," is the clearest expression of this conviction you have ever written.

Jean: Yes, I would agree with that.

The Reaper: Would you like to say anything else about it?

Jean: Yes. I would. And will! You know, amino acids are the building blocks of the self. I was reading a lot about the beginnings of the self on earth—

The Reaper: You mean the beginnings of life on earth.

Jean: Same difference. I was especially intrigued by the theory that the self may have begun in the snow fields of the Antarctic. Then I was struck! The snowy whiteness of the page, the chains of black hieroglyphics, no, the molecules—the letters were like molecules! After that, it was easy.

The Reaper: Perhaps now it's time to bring up a sore subject. *Bones Through Their Noses*.

Jean: Yes. That's a pretty sore subject, but I'm glad you brought it up. I can't understand the critical reception of my latest book. It seems to me that critics haven't even read past the title. After all, I go down to Tierra del Fuego, I look at the culture there, I try to resolve the dispute, and I come back and try to tell my countrymen about it in a book of poetry. I mean, what do people want? What did you think of the book?

The Reaper: We couldn't get past the title. Both of your careers have been notable not only for what you have written, but for where you have worked.

Sean & Jean: Oh, we don't work anymore.

The Reaper: Ah, yes! The Patton grants. Those are for five years, right?

Sean: Yes! But if you invest the money wisely, and we have, you can escape the rat race forever. Do you know what a block of condominiums in Redondo Beach, California brings in each month?

The Reaper: But you both used to teach.

Jean: Yes, all the time. Goddard, Columbia, Iowa, Missoula, Arkansas, Florida, Irvine, Dartmouth, even Ivy Tech!

Sean: Creative writing programs, creative writing teachers, they're a dead end.

Jean: Phew! We're sure glad to be out of that.

The Reaper: Surely you didn't feel that way all the years you were teaching.

Jean: As a matter of a fact, I think we did. If it hadn't been for NEA money and Guggenheim Fellowships and numerous trips to Italy, we probably would have gone nuts!

Sean:	Actually, when we got out of grad school we really wanted to go to Hollywood and write screen plays, but we didn't know anybody out there. So the only thing left was teaching. One does what one has to.
The Reaper:	But what about your students? Didn't you have any good ones?
Jean:	We really can't remember them very well!
Sean:	Hey! I'd like to talk about my new book.
The Reaper:	Sure. What's it called?
Sean:	Well, I'm calling it *Nightpickings*, and it's a whole new direction for me. After Boris died, when the spider bit him, I was sort of at a loss. I started going to an analyst, this beautiful man who was dying of cancer, and he helped me. Somewhere in my psyche, he told me, I had misplaced my space. Soon I could visualize where I had put it; my typewriter was there, my tape recorder, my computer terminal—all the things I need to write. They had been lost when my space was lost to myself, you understand, and when I found it again I found them again, and I wrote *Nightpickings*.
The Reaper:	Oh. What is the book about?
Sean:	The central metaphor is slug death. Once as a child, I was playing with friends and one of them had a bag of salt. He was sprinkling the salt onto slugs. They made a terrible mess on the sidewalk. And I was actually coerced into doing this, too. I admit that it really didn't take too much coercion. I have never admitted this to anyone publicly before, but I am secure enough in myself and my talent to do it now. Yes, I confess that I poured salt on a slug. I watched

it dehydrate before my eyes. I needed to do that, though. One needs to do what one must not do, to become an artist. Now, that's when I was six.

The Reaper:	Slug death is the central metaphor of *Nightpickings?*
Sean:	Yes, I'm a child of the turbulent sixties—just like Jean.
The Reaper:	We're sure everyone will be interested in *Nightpickings.* Jean, what kind of effect has criticism had on your own work.
Jean:	I like to read critics. After all, we're always criticizing. And criticism isn't just confined to poetry, you know. I think, for example, that the deconstructionist approach can be taken towards almost anything. Let me illustrate with an analogy. If Sean won't mind. . . Now, Sean has high blood pressure and his poetry has been accused of being rhetorically inflated. The word "inflated" interests me. So does the word "pressure." What if we were to switch them. What if we were to say Sean had inflated blood? And his poetry was rhetorically pressured?
The Reaper:	Are you suggesting that would make everything all right?
Jean:	Yes, I think I am! It's all semantics in the end. One high powered word bumps another. Why is the critic writing about you in the first place? Because he can't write about himself! That's why I love critics. I love Helen Vendler. I love Harold Bloom. And I'm happy to say they love me, too. In fact, I'll be thrilled to see what *they* say—because they've been silent for some time—about *Bones Through Their Noses.*

The Reaper:	Sean, how has the critic affected you?
Sean:	I've come full circle. In the early days, when I was first starting to write poetry after I'd met Jean, I confess to harboring bitter sentiments towards all critics. Today, like Jean, I am interested in the critical process as an art, too. Criticism, I think, approaches poetry. And poetry approaches criticism.
The Reaper:	That seems simple enough.
Jean:	They meet. They embrace.
Sean:	How true! The poem criticizes, criticism sings.
Jean:	And vice versa.
The Reaper:	You've mentioned critics who have been important to you. Have there been any poets? Any living poets?
Jean:	We like all the living poets.
Sean:	Once you meet someone, and I think we've met everyone, I think it's very hard to dislike his or her work.
Jean:	You get a personal feeling for a poet's work after you've had a drink with that person.
Sean:	So, when you see a bad review of someone you know, you take it personally. Here's an example. Just the other day I was reading a poetry journal—the editors must be young—and I noticed that they did not have a good word to say about anybody. Oh, they praised Thomas Hardy, but he's been dead forever. So I wrote a letter of protest.
Jean:	I bet they won't have the courage to publish it.
Sean:	Oh no. They're going to publish it. The problem,

however, in writing such letters, is making sure you say everything you want to. I didn't want my friends to think I'd left anyone out. So, of course, I had to mention a number of people who hadn't even been reviewed.

The Reaper: How long was your list?

Sean: Well, I used a lot of paper!

The Reaper: Let's go back to the original question. What living poets *do* you admire?

Sean & Jean: We like Daniel Halpern. He edits one hell of a magazine.

Jean: Red Warren, though people read him for the wrong reasons.

Sean: Donald Hall!

Jean: Chuck Simic, Chuck Wright, Chuck Bukowski.

Sean: Have you read M.L. Rosenthal's poems? They're very good.

Jean: So are Dick Howards's. And Dick Wilbur's. And Dick Hugo's. And look at all the memorable people he's chosen for the Yale Series. They're all good!

Sean: Stanley Kunitz is good. He keeps going and going and going. And writing those good poems. The man amazes me. He should be dead. Of course, you could say the same for Ken Rexroth or Ken Koch or Ken Hanson or Ken Rosen.

Jean: Let's not forget the women!

Sean: Right! Jorie, Marilyn, Sandy, Beth, Jane, Sharon, · Mekeel, Louise, Diane, Carolyn (she's beautiful), Linda, and the other Linda. . .

Jean:	Hey, Sean! Don't you think that's sexist?
Sean:	You're right, sugar. But everybody knows who I'm talking about. I know that doesn't excuse sexism, though. No matter how good we are, it seems we're doomed to suffer.
Jean:	That's OK, honey.
The Reaper:	You mean to say you like *all* of these poets?
Sean & Jean:	And more! We could go on!
The Reaper:	We really only have time for one more question. You're both influential young poets. Whatever you do, whatever direction you choose will have far reaching effects. Where do you hope to lead American poetry?
Jean:	I'll go first on this one. You've got to use the language of the average person, but you don't have to use his feelings. Anything you're into should be put into the poem. If you're into politics, write political poems. If you're into art history, write about art. If you're seeing a shrink, write about your shrink. Don't hide your hobbies or your habits. People want to know who you are first. Then they're interested in the words. Don't get hung up on the question of semantics. Remember your special self. Hell, the words will come.
Sean:	I can echo that. Talk like the man in the street, but don't worry about his emotions. Get involved and write about it. Work within the system, work within the form. Get to an art gallery and look at the pictures. They're worth thousands of words. The whole complex process of going crazy is something to write about. Hell, it's a prize winner! Sylvia Plath, dead 18 years, just won the Pulitzer. Of course, she's a good poet.

Jean:	One of our favorites.
Sean:	But getting back to my point. If you have a tendency to be an introvert in your poems, try, try, try to be an extrovert. People want flesh first, sound second. Stop worrying about language. You're yourself. You can talk.

I Have Seen, I Know

Dramatic monologue is the current narrative mode of poetry. Because of this *The Reaper* will use two dramatic terms to describe current contemporary narrative poetry: reaction and anticipation. For example, an actor who only anticipates is a bad actor. He has already decided how he will act, so he avoids conflict and surprise. The poet who writes hoping to strike the proper attitude—the right way his persona should speak, the right political stance—backpedals in anticipation. What he says, whether right or wrong, is predictable. In contrast, the actor who reacts engages his audience with an emotional intensity that surprises them both and would be alien and terrifying to his counterpart who can only anticipate. The poet who engages in real narration will always be surprising just as life with its emotional eruptions is always surprising.

Narrative is the most flexible of all literary forms. *The Odyssey* begins near the end of Odysseus' journey and Odysseus himself narrates many of his past adventures to Nausicaa's father Alcinous. Dante, on the other hand, takes us step by step through his Easter weekend. Both narrations are full of surprises.

In recent history, poets have decided that the one story they have to tell is the story of their lives, too often reduced, as in journalism, to only the news that's fit to print. What they really want to write are lyrics. They mistrust narration. They do not understand its flexibility. They do not comprehend the compression of narrative poetry. Narrative poetry can tell a story in less space than prose and more immediately. It gives more the sense of living the story, than standing outside of it, but only if the story is as unpredictable as life. This does not mean evasion: Look how I eluded the plot; I'm on top of things here. Look how smart I am in getting around the story. Ain't I a dandy? The dandy dresses for the occasion, practicing in front of the mirror the right things to say. He lives by anticipation; he traffics in it.

The Reaper wants to talk about four examples of narrative poetry: Randall Jarrell's "Next Day," Robert Lowell's "Thanksgiving's Over," Carolyn Forché's "Return," and Denis Johnson's "The Confession of St. Jim-Ralph." Since all the poems, except Jarrell's, are fairly long, The Reaper will quote where he can, paraphrase where he must, and assume that you know all of them well. They are dramatic monologues, and three of them clearly use a convention of that form: the persona. Jarrell's is a woman, Lowell's a man named Michael whose wife has killed herself, and Johnson's is named by the title. Forché speaks in first person, ostensibly as herself, but more as a symbol of raised consciousness.

"Next Day" is an enormously influential poem, for its use of the opposite sex as a persona, for its brand names, suburban settings, and melancholy tone, and its mixture of erudition and banality, prose rhythm and rhyme. If Lowell, as Jarrell once said, made his personae sound like Robert Lowell, this woman sounds like Jarrell. But then she is a mask. As in his criticism, here Jarrell is right on top of things; every move is perfectly calculated. Even the one startling intrusion is later accounted for.

> The slacked or shorted, basketed, identical
> Food-gathering flocks
> Are selves I overlook. Wisdom, said William James,

Is learning what to overlook. And I am wise
If that is wisdom.

After all, though the woman is choosing detergent as she does her
own shopping in the supermarket, she is well-married, educated,
and has a maid. There is an impulse to apologize for the surprise
and a commitment to smoothing it out, to making it as digestible
for the reader as one of the Cornish game hens she is buying. The
poem's emotion is meant to be supplied by the irony of a woman
meditating in a supermarket on her own aging and death the day
after her friend's funeral. For many readers the poem is quite suc-
cessful. But for *The Reaper* it is not. Here is why: the life portrayed is
really after-life; the woman is a posture who repeats all that we
would expect of her; the poet has made flesh, perhaps, in trying to
convince us he knows what this woman is thinking, but he has not
made a woman, much less a life. This is an attractive method in the
contemporary narrative for keeping the story under control, at all
costs, even at the expense of emotion. Granted, Jarrell was of a
school where irony was emotion. And that may be the problem here,
but the larger issue is the story. He has put that woman in a super-
market and she is thinking about herself with altogether too much
self-knowledge, calmly, lucidly narrating a position on her life rather
than her life.

The speaker of Forché's "Return" thinks her life has been changed.
She has seen corruption, suffering, and war in a Latin American
country and describes these things and her frustration with Ameri-
can indifference to an older friend who has seen it all before.

> Upon my return to America, Josephine:
> the iced drinks and paper umbrellas, clean
> toilets and Los Angeles palm trees moving
> like lean women, I was afraid more than
> I had been, even of motels so much so
> that for months every tire blow-out
> was final, every strange car near the house

kept watch and I strained even to remember
things impossible to forget. You took
my stories apart for hours, sitting
on your sofa with your legs under you
and fifty years in your face.

The reader, too, has seen it all before, especially the reader who sub-
scribes to newspapers and watches Dan Rather or his fellow an-
chors. Of course, Forché is not just reporting; she has an editorial
opinion, too. Her interlocutor, whom she quotes indirectly (you
said, you say), helps her define her position.

Go try on
Americans your long, dull story
of corruption, but better to give
them what they want

Since this follows a passage where Josephine says, "So you've
come to understand why / men and women of good will read / tor-
ture reports with fascination," a weird version of imitative fallacy
seems at work. If torture reports are a kind of pornography, why is
"Return" given in large measure to torture reports?

Tell them about the razor, the live wire,
dry ice and concrete, grey rats and above all
who fucked her, how many times and when.
Tell them about retaliation: Jose lying
on a flat bed truck, waving his stumps
in your face, his hands cut off by his
captors and thrown to the many acres
of cotton, lost, still, and holding
the last few lumps of leeched earth . . . reports
of mice introduced into women, of men
whose testicles are crushed like eggs.

The story here is of the speaker's political education, and reports of torture are evidently a part of it. But good narrative poetry is not simply reportage. What is its justification? Is Forché educating the reader, nominally with her own education? Or titillating the reader? Or thrashing the reader with pornographic relish? Where Jarrell was too much in control, the control Forché intends to exert wets her audience like an accidental spray of saliva.

> I go mad, for example
> in the Safeway, at the many heads
> of lettuce, papayas and sugar, pineapples
> and coffee, especially the coffee.
> And when I speak with American men,
> there is some absence of recognition:
> their constant Scotch and fine white
> hands, many hours of business, penises
> hardened by motor inns and a faint
> resemblance to their wives. I cannot
> keep going.

Neither can *The Reaper*. Nor, he assumes can any other reader who seeks a compelling narrative. It is a great pity that the suffering in El Salvador, which Forché has annexed to her reputation, should be translated into shrill political rhetoric. The writing throughout "Return" is often as inaccurate as propaganda: "penises / hardened by motor inns and a faint / resemblance to their wives." The rhythm is like throat cramps; one never knows where to take a breath. The ending is much too ambiguous for this graphic list of images.

> You have not returned to your country,
> but to a life you never left.

Maybe in a better poem, this would be a better ending. In this crippled narrative, to which there is but one correct response ("Agree with me or you're a fascist"), poetry is not the point. Unlike Jarrell who strained for the right response within the context of his poem, Forché's right response is a foregone conclusion—to her. Both poems (though in the case of "Return" *The Reaper* uses the term generously) misuse narrative.

This is not the case in "Thanksgiving's Over" because Robert Lowell is not after a right response. The poem is about a marriage. A man, Michael, remembers his late wife's insanity. It is she who speaks through most of the poem though not indirectly as the character Josephine in Forché's poem. She narrates her madness, linking it somewhat conventionally to birds ("I hear the birds inside me . . .") and, the signature of early Lowell, to St. Francis. As she reminds Michael of how she went mad, of how he had her put away, and of her suicide, the emotion breaks through saving the narrative from conventionality. In other words, at critical points in the poem she says things we would never expect her to say. A recognizable story becomes unique.

> . . . "If you're worth the burying
> And burning, Michael, God will let you know
> Your merits for the love I felt the want
> Of, when your mercy shipped me to Vermont
>
> To the Asylum. Michael, was there warrant
> For killing love? As if the birds that range
> The bestiary-garden by my cell,
> Like angels in the needle-point, my Aunt
> Bequeathed our altar-guild, could want
> To hurt a fly! . . . But Michael, I was well;
> My mind was well;
> I wanted to be loved— . . ."

Although it benefits from the power of real narrative, "Thanksgiving's Over" is by no means a perfect poem. The wife's mad chatter goes on much too long, over-freighted with the bird symbolism. But, perhaps, this contributes to the poem's ultimate strength; it's not a flabby poem, it's musclebound. Still the narrative spine running through it is unmistakable. The poem's most powerful moments would not exist without it.

> "Husband, you used to call me Tomcat-kitten:
> While we were playing Hamlet on our stage
> With curtain rods for foils, my eyes were bleeding;
> I was your valentine.
> You are a bastard, Michael, aren't you! *Nein,*
> Michael. It's no more valentines."

In its absence we would have too much control (the bird metaphor), and studied ranting and raving (the wife's madness). At times the writing is marvelously compressed ""Thanksgiving night: Third Avenue was dead; / My fowl was soupbones,") at others condensed but confusing ("Where I'd stumbled from the street, / A red cement Saint Francis fed a row/Of toga'd boys with birds beneath a Child."). The point is that Lowell's narrative discovers emotion; it does not report it. This is what all good narrative does because it is an expression of daily life where *nothing,* especially emotion, is predictable.

The best example of this among the four poems discussed here is Denis Johnson's "The Confession of St. Jim-Ralph." This is the kind of poem that precedes critical theory. It says *this is how it's done.* Only if you've had a frontal lobotomy could you fail to be moved by this poem. It is everything you will not hear on the news. It is an entire life and the stuff, without political savvy or social graces, that would embarrass dinner parties and poetry readings. It is not modulated to please.

The poem tells the story of one man's rite of passage through contemporary vocations, which are almost like incarnations—soldier, rock star, atom bomb builder, joiner and apologist, priest and prayer. The sub-title of the poem, "Our Patron of Falling Short, Who Became a Prayer," and especially the name St. Jim-Ralph with its distinctly American flavor indicate that we are about to witness a vision of our time.

"This family's full of the dead," my father told me.
I was eight. I used to make excuses
to join him in the washroom as he bathed
in the mornings, soaping himself carefully
so as not to splash the automatic pistol
wrapped in plastic he rested near to hand.
At a certain point, the sun came through the blinds
and shafted the toilet bowl, filling it with light
as he spoke of killing everyone, often taking
the pistol from its wrap and holding its mouth
against his breast, explaining that no safety
lay anywhere, unless he should shoot the fear
that stood up on its hind legs in his heart.
Such things were always on TV—I thought
that one world merged in the next, and I resolved
to win the great Congressional Medal of Honor,
to make a name on the stage, and die a priest.

In each episode, in each career, he finds the essence of each vocation. It is precisely this that usually goes unspoken in the slice-of-life poem—(. . . My comrades fled, / but I was healed by everything that happened,").

I stood at home plate, vomit on my blouse
and whiskey in my blood, and heard the dirt
of my home town falling grain by grain
out of the afternoon, while everyone's
rahrahrahs affected me like silence.
The mayor handed me a four-by-four-
inch cardboard box a colonel handed **him**:
I threw it at the vast face of the crowd,
Screaming I wanted only the Medal of Honor . . .

Going mad he "loses the thread of his existence" and wakes up in a rock and roll band.

With four monstrosities in uniforms
like mine, I pulverized guitars and wept
for the merriment of many.

However, that career, too, is a failure and his only decoration is a loss of hearing. Despite the narrative form, the poem contains a sequence of seductive chaos. This is the beauty of narrative.

Ten years I wasted all I had, and then
ten years I lived correctly—held a job
in a factory that made explosions,
where deafness was an asset. I did well,
I never missed a day, I polished late,
honed my skills, received promotions—in the end
I built explosions for atomic bombs,
forty-three I built myself, which one of these
days will deafen you, as I am deafened.
I wrenched the fraternal orders with my tale
of sorrowful delinquency—the Elks,
the Lions, Moose; those animals, they loved
the crippled rock'n'roller with the heart
wrung out as empty as his former mind,
and variously and often they cited me.
I walked the malls with an expanded chest,
took my sips with my pinkie cocked,
firing dry martinis at my larynx
and yearning for the strength of soul it takes
to suck a bullet from an actual
pistol, hating my own drained face
as I intimidated mirrors, or stood
in a jail of lies before the Eagle Scouts, . . .

Having reached a point of excruciating banality and dishonesty, he turns to God, or at least a monastery, in the wilderness.

This was my ceaseless prayer, until my lips
were muscles and my heart could talk,
telling it over and over to itself;
until they fired me and drove me to the edge
of things, and dumped my prayer into the desert.
Drinking cactus milk and eating sand,
I wandered until I saw a monastery
standing higher and higher, at first a loose
mirage, but soon more real than I was.
There I fell on my face and let light carry
me into the world—just as my uncle told it
nine million years ago when I was eight—
and the prison of my human shape exploded,
my heart cracked open and the blood poured out
over stones that got up and walked when it touched them.
High in the noon, some kind of jet plane winked
like a dime; I saw it also flashed
over the vast, perfumed, commercial places
filled with stupid but well-intentioned people,
the wreckages and ambushes of love
putting themselves across, making it pay
in the margins of the fire, in the calm spaces,
taken across the dance-floor by a last romance,
kissing softly in a hallucination strewn
with bus tickets and an originless music—
and now death comes to them, a little boy
in a baseball cap and pyjamas, doing things
to the locks of the heart. . . This was my vision.
Here I saw the truth of the horizon,
the way of coming and going in this life.
I never drifted up from my beginning:
I rose as inexorably as heat.

The final ambiguity of the poem, about the incarnation of the speaker ("I am a monk who never prays. I am / a prayer.") is a powerful one, for he is

> . . . the prayer that everything
> is praying: the summer evening a held bubble,
> every gesture riveting the love,
> the swaying of waitresses, the eleven television
> sets in a storefront broadcasting a murderer's face—
> these things speak the clear promise of Heaven.

What the poem teaches us is that the purpose of narrative is to give us the whole memorable life in as few lines as possible (262 lines is compressed compared to 262 pages of prose). Narrative is so much an extension of life and Johnson's poem shows that life is so strange and unmanageable and unpredictable that the poet who would use this form cannot have a pre-digested program. He must have a story to tell.

The "I" of the dramatic monologue gives the poem an apparent authenticity. But when this speaker is narrating a story, that element—the story—requires more than appearances. The word *story*, when it is traced back through its Indo-European roots, meets the word *veda: I have seen, I know.* We think of storytellers as witnesses, all the more so when they speak in first person and in a poem. The problem for the poet is to find how what he or she has witnessed can be relived. For as soon as the story is too well understood by the teller or, even worse, distorted to corroborate an ideology, it loses authenticity. To have a story to tell, in the magically flexible form of the narrative, means to react to life as it is lived and not as it is anticipated.

"Thanatopsis" Revisited
The Essay As Poem

To him who in the love of nature holds
Communion with her visible forms, she speaks
A various language; for his gayer hours
She has a voice of gladness, and a smile
And eloquence of beauty, and she glides
Into his darker musings, with a mild
And healing sympathy, that steals away
Their sharpness, ere he is aware. When thoughts
Of the last bitter hours come like a blight
Over thy spirit, and sad images
Of the stern agony, and shroud, and pall,
And breathless darkness, and the narrow house,
Make thee to shudder, and grow sick at heart,—
Go forth, under the open sky and list
To Nature's teachings, while from all around—
Earth and her water, and the depths of air,—
Comes a still voice—

                Yet a few days, and thee
The all-beholding sun shall see no more
In all his course; nor yet in the cold ground,

Where thy pale form was laid, with many tears,
Nor in the embrace of ocean, shall exist
Thy image. Earth, that nourished thee, shall claim
Thy growth, to be resolved to earth again,
And, lost each human trace, surrendering up
Thine individual being, shalt thou go
To mix forever with the elements,
To be a brother to the insensible rock
And to the sluggish clod, which the rude swain
Turns with his share, and treads upon. The oak
Shall send his roots abroad, and pierce thy mould.

    Yet not to thine eternal resting-place
Shalt thou retire alone, nor couldst thou wish
Couch more magnificent. Thou shalt lie down
With patriarchs of the infant world, with kings,
The powerful of the earth, the wise, the good,
Fair forms, and hoary seers of ages past,
All in one mighty sepulchre. The hills
Rock-ribbed and ancient as the sun, the vales
Stretching in pensive quietness between;
The venerable woods—rivers that move
In majesty, and the complaining brooks
That make the meadows green; and, poured round all,
Old Ocean's gray and melancholy waste,—
Are but the solemn decorations all
Of the great tomb of man. The golden sun,
The planets, all the infinite host of heaven,
Are shining on the sad abodes of death,
Through the still lapse of ages. All that tread
The globe are but a handful of the tribes
That slumber in its bosom.—Take the wings
Of morning, pierce the Barcan wilderness,
Or lose thyself in the continuous woods

Where rolls the Oregon, and hears no sound,
Save his own dashings—yet the dead are there:
And millions in those solitudes, since first
The flight of years began, have laid them down
In their last sleep—the dead reign there alone.
So shalt thou rest, and what if thou withdraw
In silence from the living, and no friend
Take note of thy departure? All that breathe
Will share thy destiny. The gay will laugh
When thou are gone, the solemn brood of care
Plod on, and each one as before will chase
His favorite phantom; yet all these shall leave
Their mirth and their employments, and shall come
And make their bed with thee. As the long train
Of ages glide away, the sons of men,
The youth in life's green spring, and he who goes
In the full strength of years, matron and maid,
The speechless babe, and the gray-headed man—
Shall one by one be gathered to thy side,
By those, who in their own turn shall follow them.

    So live, that when thy summons comes to join
The innumerable caravan, which moves
To that mysterious realm, where each shall take
His chamber in the silent halls of death,
Thou go not, like the quarry-slave at night,
Scourged to his dungeon, but, sustained and soothed
By an unfaltering trust, approach thy grave,
Like one who wraps the drapery of his couch
About him, and lies down to pleasant dreams.

Decades before Emily Dickinson and Walt Whitman began
writing the poems which have led us to think of them as Mother
and Father, William Cullen Bryant, at the age of seventeen, com-

pleted his first version of "Thanatopsis." It was 1811 and American literature, with its Western European foundation, had all its future ahead of it. Especially in poetry, there was as yet no present to speak of. "Thanatopsis," for good or ill, changed all that. Supporters hailed Bryant's poem as the clearest expression and embodiment of American freedom. The American frontier spirit was there, they claimed, and the American landscape. Detractors, on the other hand (and these came later), declared that the poem merely proved that American poets could be as pompous and sentimental as Continental poets—especially English poets. And then came Dickinson and Whitman, the best American poets of the 19th century. Naturally, contemporary poets would like to think of themselves as related to these two, but today as *The Reaper* surveys the shopping malls of poetry with their linguistic wares promoting almost unified sensibilities, he finds a more likely mother-father for them in Bryant's studied brainchild. Though the majority of contemporary American poets will, as they *think* they should, grimace when Bryant is evoked, they might be better off examining just how much they have in common with him.

The Reaper intends to focus on this intimate relationship for the sake of clarity. The historical perspective is essential here. Time and again in these pages, *The Reaper* has assailed the wares of fashion and suggested alternative ways of perceiving narrative as a way out. But just what kind of poem conforms to fashion? All of the poems but four discussed in the following pages illustrate the method and sensibility that American poets have found most sympathetic since the time of Bryant—the mediation or poem-as-essay, the loose fit for the self-absorbed sensibility. *The Reaper's* case will be presented in four parts:

1. An interpretation of "Thanatopsis," that most "contemporary" of 19th century poems.

2. An assessment of *American Poetry Review's* editorial policy as exemplified by its tenth anniversary issue.

3. Meditative poets and poems. Interpretations of representative selections from APR's tenth anniversary issue—the stepchildren of "Thanatopsis."

4. Narrative poems. Examination of the four poems from the aforementioned APR that employ narrative.

1.

Though Bryant's point of view is not acceptable to most contemporary poets, the strategy of "Thanatopsis" seems little different from one employed in the meditative poems found in literary magazines today. In Bryant's poem everything matters, and every thought expressed is predictable. In most contemporary meditative poems *nothing* matters, but the expressions of pseudo-revelations are predictable, too.

Here is the strategy of Bryant's poem. The title "Thanatopsis" means "a meditation on death." In keeping with the rhetoric of his day Bryant's speaker, in spite of the blank verse, expresses himself in the form of a sermon-essay. The precursors of this strategy are the productions of the British Graveyard School. Some scholars declare that the poem is distinctive because it embodies the sprawling American landscape and muscular spirit. If, however, there is anything in the poem that is uniquely American, *The Reaper* cannot find it. The entire life process is included, generalized, and smoothed out. Even the specter of death is injected again and again with a potent tranquilizer ("Nor couldst thou wish / Couch more magnificent"). Despite Bryant's one rebellious claim, his rejection of Calvinism (he compares death with the crumbling of the insensible clod, but even this was fashionable for a young intellectual of the period) the point of view in the poem is remarkably predictable. Even the sentimental, early Romantic conclusion (". . . approach thy grave, / Like one who wraps the drapery of his couch / About him and lies down to pleasant dreams.") adheres serenely to the popular views of Bryant's time. Of course, this sweet romanticism is utterly devoid of the decadence encountered in romantic expression today, and that is the major difference in sensibility between Bryant and his contemporary offspring. It is, however, a difference only of degree.

Besides point of view, Bryant's language is different. No reader can fail to recognize the elevated, archaic pronouns (thou, thee), the plodding metrical structure, the outdated figures of speech ("wings of morning," "the infinite host of Heaven"). Yet that was the poetic language of the time. What is important here is that the poem provides a form for the writer to tell us how he feels about death, lost love, loss, the lost, etc. The world around him is usually described in generalities: the descriptions are frequently inaccurate. Although the contemporary meditation may contain more specific language and concrete examples, it is the same grab bag. What counts are the private thoughts the poet chooses to share; reactions just doesn't matter. Bryant shields himself from emotion by pretending to know all; the contemporary meditative poet evades emotion by pretending to know nothing. In both cases, the form fits the purpose perfectly.

Is it not disturbing to consider how little things have changed? *The Reaper* finds it ironic that "Thanatopsis," the potent precursor of the dominant type of verse in America today, is itself derivative, the poor distant cousin of other, better poems.

2.

The American Poetry Review is a phenomenon: nobody likes it, but everybody reads it. Yet that dislike does not stem from any disagreement with its editorial principles, for it appears to have none. Since it is a glamour magazine, it invites jealousy. Those who have not appeared in it look at the poems and photographs of the poets who have, and hate them. And hate the magazine; and keep reading it. There it is. To argue the subtleties would be disingenuous. Everybody reads it, meaning poets and presumably people important to them. To the readers of *APR everybody* is the population of the world of poetry.

So, *APR* is a glamour magazine. If it ever had principles upon which it was based, they may have related to the imagism of the 1960's and the need to flee from it or enhance it. If so, then Stanley Plumly's "Chapter and Verse" columns in *APR* half-a-dozen years ago came as close as ever to enunciating a policy. But look back, see the poet Ai featured in an early issue—the spare, bizarre, violent imagism of her poems; see the praise for the young, successful imagist Gregory Orr in Donald Hall's "Knock, Knock" columns, also a feature of *APR*'s early years. Although the interest in translation has continued, as the contents of mainstream American poetry have subtly changed, so has *APR*. What *The Reaper* hopes to identify is what we have at the moment, as presented us by *APR*, arguably the most representative organ of American poetry today. Imagism has become enhanced; it has become speculation, moving from the thing pictured to the act of picturing itself. Not a minor difference, and one that has led to an increase in the number of words one finds in any given poem, due to the discursiveness of meditative verse. A happy reader or author might call this *fullness;* but *inflation* and *prolixity* are often appropriate descriptions, too.

American Poetry Review has had little to do with this change, except as it promotes imitation, which is not a small accomplishment. Neither is it a primary force. *APR* is merely a channel; if an earthquake changed the geography tomorrow, providing there were plenty of photographs, the magazine would accommodate itself. As it is, narrative poetry not being to the general taste at the moment, it is not to *APR*'s. However, that seems too easy an assessment, like skimming any recent issue and seeing only the pix and advertisements (nobody reads it, but everybody skims it). Narrative is still a largely untried form in American poetry. Except for a handful, the 48 poems of the tenth anniversary issue of *APR* seem oppositely charged, and if their authors approach narrative at all, it is to recoil from it as if from a mystery they cannot penetrate; the mystery to *The Reaper* is whether this is personal style or fashionable response. It appears to be both.

The pity is, that in turning away, the form they return to—the meditative poem or essay-in-verse—has played itself out. Basically it is a form little changed from Montaigne; admittedly it is superb in a master's hands. An occasion or series of occasions are contemplated and connected until they render a theme; a theme or idea presents itself through a panoply of examples; the form is more or less successful depending upon the poet's gifts, but both Shakespeare and anybody else with the knack can write a sonnet. To give this a more positive connotation, and one used occasionally in response to such poetry: these are variations on a theme or themes with variations, like music.

It is not narrative, this poetry. There is no narrative without a story. And, if a story is on the poet's mind, with this sort of approach, it remains an anecdote, a trace element, merely an undeveloped case in point. A story can only successfully be presented as narrative: that's its shape. Still, again and again, the contemporary poet is not in the mood to develop it fully; his form does not require it. Yet, when that bit of magic does erupt, as it does in almost every poem *The Reaper* plans to discuss, the poem's complexion takes on a fresher color, momentarily, before returning to its common shade.

What has *APR* contributed to this style and the poets of this style; how has it kept the mainstream flowing, both at flood level and, presently, so sluggishly that a calm of consensus seems to have come over the face of it? Variety seemed to be an original aim of the editors, and still does, but only as a disguise. Publish the pictures of poets and other authors, the reviewers and critics, too, to show how different they all look from one another. Good idea. That is, until the poets learned to pose; granted, most pictured are Americans who can't help it if they want to be movie stars; even if their models for such pix are older poets of the original pictorial anthologies, the Hollywood pout and sneer are everywhere evident. Well, it seemed like a good idea. Another was to put out feelers nationally and internationally for whatever was going on and put it on their

pages; for in its early days, *APR* was partly intended as a trade jour-
nal and to this day it functions that way. But word of mouth has a
way of being the bias of personalities, and again, without any prin-
ciples, whatever filters in from out there can be tainted by prejudices
apart from poetry. Still, we may respond heartily, when was it not
so? Well, maybe not heartily.

On closer inspection, though, there's nothing different in these
aims than we would find in the new *Vanity Fair*, itself sadly given over
to big pix and superficial prose (in the latter case about writers like
Elizabeth Hardwick and V. S. Pritchett who could have written
much better notes on themselves than they get). One, too, could
point to *Rolling Stone*, yet this analogy is perfectly obvious, a cause for
levity (*Rolling Poem*), and clearly invited by the editors (maybe format
was their only principle). Yet before *Rolling Stone* became supermar-
ket respectable, it was a place for a small set of rock'n'roll aficionados
to talk about a most unrespectable kind of music; it, too, had and
still has attributes of the trade journal. But was respectability always
Rolling Stone's aim? If not, then maybe it just sort of happened. It's
already an old story, anyway (how American that aging process is!).
Was *APR's* aim to make poetry respectable enough for supermarkets,
too?

The tenth anniversary issue, despite the photos, the line-up of
established poets, the plethora of ads, the very format itself, says
one thing: once some people got together to publish what they
liked, without rhyme or reason, at a time when both rhyme and rea-
son were out of favor, like principles and standards and dogma.
Unfortunately, the editors of *APR* read their own magazine. In the
second half of its life, *APR* has become one with the type of poetry
it unwittingly promotes, and both have become more so. It has kept
the stream going, like many another magazine of taste in this coun-
try, where one or more editors have said—"we're just going to pub-
lish what we like"—as if this mystery made each taste distinct; *de
gustibus* has become a complacent verity.

In the age of taste, editorial policy does consist of saying only "I like it." Since there is a give-and-take between the purveyors of the arts and the artists themselves (more so than between artists and critics), what is liked will be imitated—and so on. But that is a picture of poetry's evolution in the small; a larger picture, the one *The Reaper* hopes to make clear, is of a superficial variety of styles, backgrounds, schools, when beneath is a unity that would surprise many, especially those who perceive conspiracies, axes of power, and cliques.

The unity is one of method: poetry has become meditative in form, having surrendered the narrative to prose. Granted it has been a considerable time since poetry's grip on narrative was truly sure, despite Frost who now appears as much an anomaly in our time as George Crabbe was in his. However, even regarding one of the recent best of this movement, Elizabeth Bishop, all one needs to do to stand in the presence of narrative's superior power is to read "The Moose" in her last book *Geography III.* If *The Reaper* argues that it is her greatest poem, he trusts readers will understand the basis of his judgement. Could the editors of *APR* argue their preference for any of the poems published in the tenth anniversary issue?

The Reaper has decided to do them a favor and explain their prejudices to them, if not their principles. Actually, these terms, *prejudice* and *principle,* are extrapolated from Allen Tate's 1936 essay "The Function of a Literary Quarterly." Tate argues, of course, for the necessity of established critical principles; he even attempts to scour the negative connotation from the word *dogma* (easy for a Roman Catholic maybe; harder for others). After making the connection between principle and dogma, he states

> . . . it must be remembered that prejudice is not dogma, that the one has no toleration for the other. If prejudice were dogma, *The New York Times Book Review* would be a first-rate critical organ.

Fashion prejudices *APR* in favor of meditative verse; it is not alone, either; as *The Reaper* has said, it is merely the most representative. It is finally a superficial comment to say American poetry all sounds alike, for personalities do differ, so do talents. What concerns *The*

Reaper is the consensus below, in the depths, where form resides. There, all modes are unified. There is one preferred way of writing a poem in America today. All *APR* says—and no doubt it is fully capable of saying something different—all it says right now is "We like it."

3.

Twenty-one poets have contributed 48 poems to the tenth anniversary issue of *APR*. The poets appear in alphabetical order, which is how they will be discussed in this section. *The Reaper* is interested in no more than half of the poems except for the four narratives to be discussed in the final section of this essay; the others represent much meditative verse, but also use narrative itself as an optional strategy, something to set a scene, to frame an illustration, even to think over, sometimes accidentally, but never to commit oneself to.

Four poems by Marvin Bell are included, and ironically for *The Reaper's* purposes, the first is called "A True Story." In fact, its form is largely narrative, and its story is constructed to beguile and to amuse. In the end, the situation produces a punch-line, and the poem resonates as a joke, a shaggy dog story, an anecdote about mistaking pieces of a chandelier found in a Roman hotel room for diamonds, then finding a men's magazine with pages stuck together and making no mistake about **it**. The speaker of the poem puts things back where he found them, wittily averring, "so too everyone / who, when in Rome, / will do what the Romans do."

This is not what *The Reaper* is speaking of when referring to narrative poetry. This poem uses narrative for its suspenseful charm; for all has been preconceived to point to two fine turns—the transition between its two stanzas, revealing that the jewels are not what they seem, and the poem's use of cliché to conclude. To illustrate further the difference between this and narrative poetry, another poem called "How I Got the Words" actually comes closer to the magnetism of narrative. Describing how he lost a letter out of a window, the speaker decides he will try to find it.

> So I let a second paper go
> through the slot and into the hand of the wind. . .
> I followed to your letter the blank page
> which landed exactly next to it . . .

Something about this following after, this search, shows a faith in narrative missing from "A True Story." Either the form is not Bell's strength or he does not trust it, for he ends "How I Got the Words" with a complicated simile which undercuts the simple ingenuity of the motion he has followed. To read Bell at his best is to read "Against Stuff." Here he is at ease.

> The beauty that goes up in flame
> is touchable beauty—the beauty of things
> in light; of all manner of representing
> people, mouths open or closed forever;
> and of beauty known by its shape
> in the dark, or by whatever hides and reveals it—
> beauty received, registered,
> the object of study, talent and abandon.

"Abstinence" by Richard Cecil sounds like the atmospheric beginning of a psychological short story or novel, perhaps about an obsession that has turned the narrator's life upside down; either he is beginning the story before or after the event.

> Years ago I sipped three drinks
> every evening in the thickening shade
> and felt the sunshine spread across my skin
>
> about the time of the rising of the moon
> through dense clouds over dark hills,
> lighting them as much as sun at dawn.

I happened to reverse life's normal cycle.
Instead of sleep and work and recreation
determined by the angle of the sun

I rose to the level of the gin each night
and set with the setting of my martini glass
into the lukewarm water in the dishpan.

He has ten more stanzas to go, but not much more is going to hap-
pen. This condition itself, this mood, is the focus of the meditation.
Narratively, "I happened to reverse life's normal cycle" has poten-
tial, and yet the anti-cycle is described, brooded over, and if there's
a story it is glazed over: "I assumed at first that I was dreaming."
Watching others leave their work as his, which is drinking, begins,
he imagines at the center of the city where they work a "deep, cold
lake." An interesting conceit, coming near the poem's end, and alto-
gether appropriate, for as an object of meditation it symbolizes the
unity of purpose in the essay-as-poem. "Abstinence" itself is a tan-
talizing preface that serves as a poem. Just as the dramatic mono-
logue has dispensed with the drama, similarly contemporary poetry
has dispensed with the story, offering fragments of the former whole.

It is a sober matter to read meditations like Cecil's and even
Bell's, though Bell's humor is distinct, and when he is not trying to
puncture somebody's else's bubble, he wears his own learning lightly.
Albert Goldbarth is famously witty, both in the metaphysical and
comic sense. His "Halos" shows what talent is needed to make
changes on one subject really ring, even without going anywhere.
Here, narrative is enough to set the occasion.

Sometimes, lumbering back to bed
from the bathroom, I think of the cedars of Lebanon, also
heavy in body and moving
slow through time, and by the pun,
the "lumber," made my brothers.

The story here is all about thinking, though; thus it is in every meditative poem. If a poem's about thinking, it had better be interesting; it had better go down in an order that surprises and gives pleasure with its connections. From this beginning, Goldbarth leaps to a clever disquisition on halos, both secular and sublime.

> Janice Landry
> 20, graduate student, art history, who'd maybe
> never been to church in her life, took the blaze
> from the slide projector full upon her hair
> with a subtler aurora than the Virgin's.
>
> In Fra Angelico,
> angels bear their smithied medallions effortlessly,
> herds of palominos whose manes are a substance
> wholly ethereal.

All very enjoyable, fun, and in the growing anthology of poems about painting, "Halos" includes one of the most memorable observations: "Leonardo's / figures glow as if holiness were health." But there is a sadness, too, to see Janice Landry slip away as she does:

> If she wasn't my first she was my
> first with a grace that was greater than we were.
> Lumbering back from washing her glaze off my cock,
> I'd feel a part of the air.

She is discarded so solipsistically, so like the story of which she is a part, that it is difficult to enjoy the poem's real virtues. However, that is the sort of poem this is, since flotsam and jetsam are what the current market bears; if solipsism is a failure of many contemporary poems, it is time to look at the form of the meditation itself.

At the heart of the issue is the present master of the form. Nowhere else are they more manifest—the successes and the symptoms of the contemporary essay-as-poem. Jorie Graham's "The Sense of an Ending" indicates the poet's preferences in its title; to call the poem only "An Ending" would imply a narrative; in fact, it would call for one. Echoing Frank Kermode and adding "the sense of" releases her from that restriction and grants her admittance to the thinking room of meditation. She can begin by linking phenomena thematically.

> There in the sound of the chainsaw winding down. The crack
> of the young trees a distant
>
> neighbor needs to clear. A slamming
> door. The freeway whining when the wind
>
> turns down this way. There in the undulant cawing way above
> of four ravens crossing back over
>
> now it's dusk (Somewhere for them is *in*
> or *out*. Therefore they point that way)...

Note how that narrative grace note—*now it's dusk*—is plangently and necessarily, it should be added, suppressed by the phenomenological insight about the birds; it's an example of how Graham's wit works.

For she is, like Bell and Goldbarth, a poet of wit, of connections, though she never goes for laughs. She ranges widely in this poem, from local to continental, commonplace to sublime senses of endings, without ever leaving the home base, her theme. And where her language is weakest, it is as much a personal tic as a flaw of the form, although one the form readily admits.

> As in the dark those small creatures
> who are blind by day awaken because this is their
>
> opening, this dark blue real in which a sound is
> a motive, in which a scent
>
> is the edge of flesh, or itself, a flesh,
>
> in which something is chosen yet nothing excluded.

Yet, this movement from vaguely resonant particulars to resonantly vague generalizations is both the aberration and indication of her writing.

Finally, in this poem, the paradox manifests itself acutely as a story, "from childhood", seems to begin.

> from childhood I still own the mornings at the poly-
> clinic, the avenue of palms always in their warm
>
> clattery wind. And the simple task, tuesdays and thursdays
> with the eyemachines: 2 of each earthly thing, one to
>
> each eye (rabbit or trumpet, apple
> or rock) and the mind
>
> given the task: to bring them
> together.

After the mind is given its task, the tense shifts to the present, and even though the past is returned to seven lines later, it becomes pain-fully obvious what the story and its form are to such a poet: another object of meditation. When she writes

> An act
> here or there like ice over the long water is said
>
> *to change the course of the story. . .*

the turn is deft, but for *The Reaper* all too familiar.

Donald Hall's "Great Day in the Cows' House" enjoys the context provided by his book *Kicking the Leaves;* knowing that book, we know where this poem takes place or can guess intelligently that it is related to the farm which provides the setting of many of that book's poems. Here the farmer, the old man who "strokes / white braids of milk, *strp, strp* from ruminant beasts" seems the familiar figure from "The Naming of Horses." So this poem benefits from an extratextual form, but it quickly announces its location *in* meditation. For despite the opening appearances, and fine narrative sequences throughout the poem, it resides stilly in a *now* that is a meditation or a thinking-over of the past, figuratively presented as "the great day."

> In the dark tie-up seven huge Holsteins
> lower their heads to feed, chained loosely to old saplings
> with whitewashed bark still on them.
> They are long dead; they survive, in the great day
> that cancels the successiveness of creatures.

Narration is succession. *The Reaper* thanks Hall for helping him to define it. Where the beauties of Jorie Graham's poem are juxtapositions and thematically relevant evocations, here they are images, pleasures for the senses.

> —Sweet bellowers enormous and interchangeable,
> your dolorous ululations
> swell out barnsides, fill spaces inside haymows,
> resound down valleys. Moos of revenant cattle
> shake ancient timbers and timbers still damp with sap.

And sequences that do occur within the stasis of memory finally have the same place here as do similar ones in Goldbarth's "Halos."

> Pull down the spiderwebs! Whitewash the tie-up's wood!
> In the great day there is also the odor of poverty,
> and anxiety over the Agricultural Inspector's visit.
> Although his ankle turns as he climbs the hill, udders
> swell for milking; his chest pains him but cows hunger.
> Then his neighbor discovers him at eighty-seven, his head
> leaning into the side of his last Holstein. . .

Although more care weighs heavily here and makes this poem read with a difference, its object is announced in the title, and any stories that come to mind, like the one above, are in service to something other than themselves.

Many would agree that Richard Hugo has a strong narrative inclination, and therefore might be readily referred to as a narrative poet. Two of the four poems included show that he understood that the most potent characteristic of a subject was the story behind it; for him it was usually the story of a place. However, "Asheville" becomes neither fish nor fowl as a meditation about whether Thomas Wolfe was right or not about coming home again, because it skims over a most intriguing story based on a presumption about a young guide to Wolfe's home. Differently, "Making Certain It Goes On" declines too glibly into knowingness. All the same, we see that Hugo cared for the story's form in a way many of those already spoken of as they are represented in this issue of *APR* do not. However, two of *The Reaper*'s favorite poems are simple, straightforward, meditative, companion pieces—"Red Stone" and "Gray Stone."

If underwater, a glowing red stone
is always good luck. Fish it out, even
if you must wade and wet your good shoes. . .
Use it for what it can do.
When it has done its work, return it softly
where you found it, and let your wet feet
sting a moment in the foam's white chill.

"Red Stone"

A gray stone does not change color wet
or dry. Baked on a scorched road or shaded
by cedars, underground or tossed
into a bright green sky, it's always gray. . .
Keep one gray stone
in a secret place, and when those you love
are broken or gone, listen
with a sustained, with a horrible attention
to the nothing it has always had to say.

"Gray Stone"

Both these talismanic poems are successions, and like Bell's "How I Got the Words" faintly reflect that form *The Reaper* keeps naming and believes, when present, has an undeniable power.

Simplicity is not always a virtue, but given the often arbitrary range of meditative verse, the two Hugo poems are refreshing, although their limit again seems set not only by their subjects but by a hint of narrative form. Marcia Southwick's "Boarded Windows" and "Why the Rain Is Ignored" benefit, too, from limitation. In the former, it is because a litany keeps it in check.

> Will I die while thinking of
> dull gray houses in the rain. . .
> Will I die while thinking of
> apples rotting on the kitchen table. . .

The thoughts following each refrain are kept from going on too long because the repetition would be lost; towards the end of the poem a new refrain, "the secret is," begins. Part of the poem's success might be a complete avoidance of narrative form, for in "Why the Rain Is Ignored," in the middle where so often a poem goes slack, a promising though threatening moment begins.

> Once, I stood in a spring fog
> after hearing the news of a friend's disappearance
> I can't recall exactly how I felt,
> but the jonquils on the lawn seemed uncomplicated
> as they tipped their heads
> in the sluggish, gray air
> and a few pink blossoms fell easily from the magnolias,
> as if the trees were unafraid
> of their own nakedness.
> Maybe we are part of a long story. . .

With that idea or thought, the story itself is lost, lost to comment, to self-consciousness, to the act of meditation—call it what you will. The rain is ignored because it is one of a succession of events.

If she wanted to, Maura Stanton could tell a good story. This is not a facile distinction between her and the others here; some of them hint that they could, too (Goldbarth, Graham) but don't want to; others (Cecil, Southwick) perhaps could not. But again, all are so far from what narrative requires, any gift for it may have atrophied. Anyway, one could not tell that Stanton has any narrative gift from "Wildlife Calendar," probably the most occasional of the poems in the issue, yet one of the most representative, too. She, more than others, states her intention explicitly; there is no feinting in another direction. Having meditated, sometimes monotonously, on each month of the calendar from January to November and its attendant wildlife picture, she writes, "And now I've reached the end of speculation." What is important is lost way back at the first line: "I read my fortune in this calendar." There is a "hint of impending form" as Charles Wright calls it in "Link Chain" (itself a non-narrative poem with narrative highlights). Yet the fortune she reads month by month is static, unsuccessive, not narrative (except as she flips pages), ending in a December snowstorm where

> The panting elk see only the blurred trees
> Along their nearest way. Not a hoofprint
> Exists behind them as they hurry forward
> Over the invisible grass of next spring.

It is in "At the Cochise Tourist Pavilion" that the problem of narrative is more clearly unsolved. A poem of 110 lines, it attenuates further and further in meditation; one can even chart this transformation according to the beginning of the poem's 27 sentences.

> Yesterday I saw my first mirage. . .
> The image lasted for miles. Astonished
> I searched my map for explanations. . .
> Of course I've seen the highway mirages. . .
> Wasn't this an illusion? Shading my eyes
> I turned the lovely water into caliche. . .

But then I felt a chill. I could imagine
Some old prospector leaning down to view
The image of his own inverted face. . .
At the tourist pavilion, under a glass case,
I found the chart of ancient Lake Cochise. . .
The old travelers had seen this same mirage.
And even Coronado may have crossed the ghost water. . .

The air conditioned air stroked my face. . .
I'd been seeing backward (Eight thousand years!). . .
All I discovered then was the roar of jets. . .

I remembered that famous doodle, or riddle,
Five ghosts looking into a pond,
Which I liked to draw in notebooks as a child. . .
I used to sympathize with those ghosts. . .
The first year or so after I don't exist,
If I could feel, I'd feel about like this. . .
I saw my own head deep inside the glass. . .
The old nun who taught biology
Seemed to be breathing at my elbow then
As if I were back in my girls' school. . .
Once she lectured on the mystery of the body. . .
She made us
Find the floating rib under our blouses. . .
We were totally new every seven years. . .

Even then I'd speculate about the brain. . .
I was already bleak and diluted. . .
The father holding his daughter's hand
May have smiled to see me staring at myself. . .
I saw I'd drawn a circle in the dust
Powdering the display case. . .
Driving home, again the shining lake
Stretched so clearly under the sun I gasped. . .

The old nun who taught biology appears when the poem is more than half over, and provides a refreshment—narrative, of course— that the poem needs there. Otherwise, each of these sentences is enhanced so that in the end all link thematically to form a speculative essay.

Finally, just as Stanton is curious in her disavowal of narrative, Gerald Stern is interesting in his oblique approach. Again, narrative is not the aim, not an accomplishment in itself, and the fundamental distrust of it shared by these poets is exhibited in Stern's sidelong entry. "Christmas Sticks" begins altogether arbitrarily, with a gratuity so contrived it is laughable.

> Before I leave I'll put two sticks on the porch
> so they can talk to each other about poor Poland. . .

Stern is noted for his good humor; perhaps, laughter is invited. In any event, we have an oblique access to Polish history, past and present, specifically focused on a wedding in some year when these sticks, becoming actors or Poles,

> . . . live out the dream of 1830, and the dream
> of 1863, the Russians gone,
> the Germans gone, the life remade, the flags
> flying over the factories, workers dancing
> above the trees, a wedding under a walnut,
> the food amazing, the last memory the bride's
> father in white showing his empty pockets. . .

Stern has some big statements to pack around the simple wedding, and though he puts them indirectly in the mouths of the two stick people, some are more believable than others.

> . . . the two of them
> walking home at night after the wedding
> talking to each other again about Pulaski
> and Casimir the great and Copernicus

and what it could have been if only sticks
had ruled the vicious world, remembering again
the Jews arriving from Spain, the scholars of Europe
descending on Cracow, half the Italian painters
living in Poland, the gentry reading books,
the women drawing and playing flutes . . .
both of them weeping for the huge carp
frozen in mud, and both of them toasting the bride.

The history is balanced on these two, like plates on dowels, and ex-
cept for the phoney sympathy for the carp, the poem bears the
reader along in a rush; to the end—don't let those plates fall! Still,
The Reaper leans forward to learn about the wedding, about that
story, and is still waiting as the two sticks are turned into abstrac-
tions: "two great masters of suffering and sadness / singing songs
about love and generation."

"The Same Moon Above Us" uses Ovid's exile and career to fur-
nish a context for what is a laboriously long rumination about the
fates both of "a man sleeping over the grilles / trying to get some
heat for his poor stomach" and the poet himself. The operative verb
is "to think" (it and its synonyms are prominent in other poems in
the issue). And yet the poem lacks the rhythmical litany of "to die"
in Marcia Southwick's poem. In fact, a tedium grows here, as in
Stanton's "Wildlife Calendar."

The question, of course, is if this tedium is more characteristic
of meditative verse than narrative. Actually, it is simply the failure
of overwriting and, in this particular case, overreaching. It would be
stretching to ascribe this flaw to one form and not the other; lying,
too.

Is one's own nature a sin? These poets speak the language they grew
up with. *APR's* involvement in this is one of reinforcement. Nothing
succeeds like success, they might answer. That is precisely why *The
Reaper* wants to redefine everything, including a poem's success.

Now *The Reaper* will turn to the four narrative poems mentioned earlier from the same issue of *APR*. Remember the numbers—four out of 48 poems. This alone is a disturbing indication of the lack of confidence contemporary poets have in the narrative. Of the following poems, two, "Portrait of a Lady" by Michael Ryan and "You Sort Old Letters" by Robert Penn Warren, provide conventional examples of narrative. The third poem, "1974: My Story in a Late Style of Fire," by Larry Levis, is a potent narrative marred by the affectations of mannerism—the flourishes of contemporary fashion. Only the fourth poem, "The Hug" by Tess Gallagher, closely approximates the kind of narrative which most interests *The Reaper*. Together these poems demonstrate the flexibility of the narrative; they also demonstrate the ways in which the narrative can break down.

Michael Ryan's "Portrait of a Lady" is a poem of eight quatrains and is preceded by a quote from Doris Lessing's *The Golden Notebook*. Here is the quote: ". . . because she was in that state so many young girls go through—a state of sexual obsession that can be like a sort of trance." Basically, this tells the story in advance. If the poem succeeds, then the quote in unnecessary. Furthermore, its inclusion intrudes on the reader and may even suggest that the poet ultimately mistrusts the strategy he has chosen. Mistrust it or not, for six stanzas Ryan manages to tell the story of an adolescent girl by focusing, conventionally, on her sexual awakening. Here is the first stanza.

> Was it only the new, old chemical stirrings
> that caused her to shoplift purple corduroys
> and squeeze into them out of her mother's hearing
> to discover what noises could come from boys?

For five subsequent stanzas Ryan's narrator impartially, though selectively, tells the girl's story, the scope of which has been determined and restricted before the telling. This is a cautious execution of narrative, but it is narrative nevertheless. It is successful, too, as long as the poet faithfully renders the girl's experience. Stanza six, for example, is dramatic:

> Then one day there was a stranger playing Space Invaders
> whose fury charged his body like a thick, hot wire.
> And she'd meet him there and do anything he told her
> Until for no reason he didn't show up anymore.

The specificity of the stranger playing Space Invaders, the girl's surrender to his violent desire, the implication of her disappointment ("for no reason") when he doesn't see her anymore, are believable.

In the last two stanzas, however, Ryan's narrator sacrifices a desirable distance from the actual story and becomes more visible.

> This is the time she marked as her awakening,
> the slow hours picking through the heart's rubble
> and finding only bits of incomprehensible pain.
> Then *she* broke hearts, got a teacher in trouble,
>
> and never gave herself easily to anyone again.
> But cruelty was a drug she needed less with age.
> She read books, became accomplished, and had children.
> At the end, at the foot of her bed, was the damage.

The narrator intrudes on the story in order to judge it. "This is the time she marked as her awakening" is arbitrary and inaccurate. Is the girl in stanzas one through six capable of such self-awareness? "The slow hours picking through the heart's rubble / and finding only bits of incomprehensible pain" is melodramatic and all too reminiscent of popular poetic pronouncements of emotional ruin. "Then *she* broke hearts"—why the italics? Does this somehow set her apart? Doesn't *everyone* break hearts? The second half of that line, "got a teacher in trouble," smacks of expository gossip and seems best

suited for a caption in *The National Enquirer*. Lines one and three of
the last stanza summarize and dismiss the subsequent experiences.
Line two is oddly ambiguous, an irksome anchor in the coda of this
poem; line four contains the girl's condemnation by the narrator, it-
self a method of dismissal. The last line also turns back on the
Jamesian title and injects it with irony.

The Reaper commends Ryan for writing a narrative that holds to-
gether from start to finish, but he is made to feel uneasy by evidence
that the poet does not quite trust his method. This evidence—the
ironic title, the explanatory quotation, the need to involve the narra-
tor arbitrarily in another character's story, the urge to comment—is
the detritus of the contemporary sensibility that does not compre-
hend the power of narrative. Still, in "Portrait of a Lady" Michael
Ryan displays a better understanding of that power than most other
poets his age.

Robert Penn Warren, of course, combines narrative and medita-
tion perhaps better than any poet writing today. The problem with
this strategy, and Warren knows it well, is keeping meditation in
harness to the story. That is where the poet's faith should lie. To sack
the narrative for the sake of meditation is to accept defeat.

In "You Sort Old Letters" Warren uses the second person to
capture a sense of immediacy that usually eludes the impartial third
person narrator. In addition, it avoids the first person narrator's ten-
dency to degenerate into confession. The plot of the poem is this:
a character, sorting through old letters, comes upon one written by
a woman with whom he had an affair years ago.

> . . . yes, yes, that tease
> Of a hostess and you, withdrawn beyond dunes, lay,
> The laughter far off, and for contact
> Of tongue and teeth, she let you first loosen a breast.
> You left town soon after—and now wonder what
> Might that day have meant.

The memory provides an occasion to meditate on choices made, on surrender and loss, on aging, on what might have been. If, like *The Reaper*, you detect an uncanny resemblance to Michael Ryan's "Portrait of a Lady," you are keeping up! Though Warren's poem is limited by its subject (the affair, after all, was a one-day stand) it is more spontaneous than Ryan's. This is true because Warren has more confidence in the narrative. He does not have to pronounce judgement (though he may imply it). Instead, he realizes that he must give faithful reactions to the story as it unfolds. For the most part he succeeds, yet the narrative is further restricted by the conventional inclusion of expository prose. Here is most of the fifth stanza.

> Of course, she had everything—money, looks,
> Wit, breeding, a charm
> Of defenseless appeal—the last what trapped, no doubt,
> The three near middle-aged fall guys, who got only
> Horns for their pains. Yes, she threw all away.
> And as you've guessed, by struggling
> Sank deeper and deeper into
> A slough of self-hate.

This is reportage. Notice how the language lets down in this stanza, as it does in Ryan's concluding stanzas. Such lapses are not ultimately fatal in narrative, but *The Reaper* insists that they are undesirable because they distract the reader's attention away from the story.

Finally, "You Sort Old Letters" and "Portrait of a Lady" are two of a kind. The wrinkle that Warren adds to the form is, as we have seen, the use of the second person. This allows the narrator to comment on the meditative process as it develops in the central character. Also, in the context of the poem it keeps the narrator out of himself. Though both of these poems are conventional in scope and execution, they do serve as examples of narrative strength. Unlike their 44 counterparts in the tenth anniversary pages of *APR*, they are concerned with the world at large and not merely with the world inside.

"1974: My Story in a Late Style of Fire," by Larry Levis extends narrative beyond the conventional boundaries just discussed. In terms of breadth of vision, it is by far the most fascinating and memorable poem printed in the issue. However, the telling of the story is marred by the mannerist gestures of contemporary fashion. Because the story itself is so good, because the lapses are so classically contemporary, *The Reaper* will reprint the entire poem and italicize what he perceives as unnecessary. Read the original as it is printed, then read it again omitting the italics. *The Reaper* believes that his version is the superior narrative poem.

When*ever* I listen to Billie Holliday, I am reminded
That I, too, was banished from New York City.
Not because of drugs or because I was interesting enough
For any *wan, overworked* patrolman to worry about—
His expression *usually a great,* gauzy spiderweb *of bewilderment*
Over his face—I was banished from New York City *by a woman.*
Sometimes, after we had stopped laughing, I would look
At her & see a cold note of *sorrow or* puzzlement go
Over her face as if someone else was *there,* behind it
Not laughing at all. We were, *I think,* in love. *No, I'm sure.*
If my house burned down tomorrow morning, & if I & my wife
And son stood looking on at the flames, & if, then,
Someone stepped out of crowd *of bystanders*
And said to me: "Didn't you once know . . . ?" No. But if
One of the flames, rising up in the scherzo of fire, turned
All the windows blank with light, & if that flame could speak,
And if it said to me: "You loved her, didn't you?" I'd answer,
Hands in my pockets, "Yes." *And then I'd let fire & misfortune*
Overwhelm my life. Sometimes, remembering those days,
I watch a *warm,* dry wind bothering a *whole* line of elms
And maples along a street in this neighborhood *until*
They're all moving at once, until I feel just like them
Trembling & in unison. *None of this matters now,*
But I never felt alone all that year, & if I had sorrows,

I also had laughter, *the affliction of angels and children.*
Which can set a house on fire if you'd let it. And even then
You might still laugh to see all of your belongings set you free
In one long choiring *of flames* that sang only to you—
Either because no one else could hear them, or because
No one else wanted to. And, mostly, because they know.
They know such music cannot last, & that it would
Tear them apart if they listened. In those days,
I was, in fact, already married, just as I am now,
Although to another woman. And that day I could have stayed
In New York. I had friends there. I could have strayed
Up Lexington Avenue, or down to Third, & caught a faint
Glistening of the sea between the buildings. But I wanted
To touch her nakedness everywhere, until her body was, again,
A bright field, or until we both reached some thicket
As if at the end of a lane, *or at the end of all desire,*
And where we could, *therefore,* be alone again, *& make*
Some dignity out of loneliness. As mostly, people cannot do.
Billie Holliday, *whose life was shorter & more humiliating*
Than my own, would have understood all this, *if only*
Because even in her late addiction & her bloodstream's
Hallelujahs, she, too, sang often of some affair, of someone
Gone, *& therefore, permanent.* And sometimes she sang
For nothing, *even then, &* it isn't anyone's business, if she did.
That morning, when she asked me to leave, wearing only
That apricot tinted, fraying camisole, *I wanted to stay.*
But I also wanted to go, to lose her suddenly, almost
For no reason & certainly without any explanation.
I remember looking down at a pair of *singular* tracks
Made in light snow the night before, at how they were
Gradually effacing themselves beneath *the tires*
Of the morning traffic, & thinking that my only other choice
Was fire, *ashes, abandonment, solitude. All of* which happened
Anyway, & soon after, & by divorce. *I know this isn't much,*

But I wanted to explain this life to you, even if
I had to become, over the years, someone else to do it.
You have to think of me what you think of me. I had
To live my life, *even its late, florid style.* Before
You judge this, think of her. Then think of fire,
Its laughter, *the music of splintering beams & glass.*
The flames reaching through the second story of a house
Almost as if to, mistakenly, rescue someone who
Left you years ago. It is so American, fire. So like us.
Its desolation. And its eventual, brief triumph.

The tale here, on the surface, is similar to Warren's in "You Sort
Old Letters." The speaker in the poem remembers an affair that oc-
curred years ago. But this poem possesses a strategy rare in contem-
porary narrative. The narrator is able to make the leap from the
personal to the collective experience. *The Reaper* refers here to the
poet's ability to perceive how his narrator's experience (if conveyed
in the first person, as in this poem it is) takes its place among the
experience of others. The unlikely but successful references to Billie
Holliday for the sake of comparison provide an example. This cat-
alyst for the telling of the story comes to the narrator from with-
out and is coupled with an interior impetus, imagining his house
destroyed by fire. Who can fail to appreciate the sophistication, the
daring scope, of this strategy when compared to Warren's stock cat-
alyst—the sorting through old letters? However, Levis in his poem,
like Ryan in his, is afflicted by equivocation.

Consider the editing done by *The Reaper*. It is based on the con-
viction that only the story is worth the telling. Meditation, if it ex-
ists, must be in service to that story; it must not obscure it. To begin
with, the title itself is obscure, pungent with the fruits of fashion.
"My Story of Fire" is the tale Levis has to tell. The year is irrele-
vant, and "in a Late Style" is merely a nod (repeated twice in the
poem—"Because even in her late addiction. . .", "To live my life,
even its late, florid style") to the posture of humorless exhaustion

that is so much in vogue today. It is a posture that intrudes on the story. It hinders the telling. This equivocation crops up throughout the poem ("Sometimes," "I think—No, I'm sure," "None of this matters now," "I wanted to stay. But I also wanted to go." "I know this isn't much"), and provides clear indications that the poet does not fully trust the story he is telling. He almost, at such moments, seems to be apologizing for asking the reader to experience genuine emotion.

The Reaper asserts that this posture is unnecessary because the story Levis has to tell, the way he tells it when sticking faithfully to narrative, is strong enough to carry its own weight. The language of self-destructive meditation is rhetorical and boring, and a poet of Levis' proven narrative gifts does not need it.

Finally, Tess Gallagher's "The Hug" comes closest to the kind of narrative *The Reaper* is seeking.

> A woman is reading a poem on the street
> and another woman stops to listen.
> We stop too, with our arms around each other.
> The poem is being read and listened to
> out here in the open. Behind us
> no one is entering or leaving houses.
>
> Suddenly a hug comes over me and I'm
> giving it to you, like a variable star shooting light off
> to make itself comfortable, then
> subsiding. I finish but keep on holding you.
> A man walks up to us and we know he hasn't come out of
> nowhere, but if he could, he
> would have. He looks homeless because of how he needs.
> "Can I have one of those?" he asks you, and I feel you
> nod. I'm surprised, surprised you don't tell him
> how it is—that I'm yours, only
> yours, etc., exclusive as a nose to

its face. Love—that's what they call it, love
that nabs you with "for me
only" and holds on.

So I walk over to him and put my arms
around him and try to
hug him like I mean it. He's got an overcoat on
so thick I can't feel him
past it. I'm starting the hug and thinking, "How big
a hug is this supposed to be ? How long
shall I hold this hug?" Already
we could be eternal, his arms falling over my
shoulders, my hands not
meeting behind his back, he is so big!
I put my head into his chest and snuggle in.
I lean into him. I lean my blood
and my wishes into him. He stands for it. This
is his and he's starting to give it back so well
I know he's getting it. This hug. So truly,
so tenderly we stop having arms and I don't know
if my lover has walked away or what, or
if the woman is still reading the poem, or the houses—
what about them? The houses.

Clearly, a little permission is a dangerous thing
But when you hug someone you want it
to be a masterpiece of connection,
the way the button on his coat
will leave the imprint of a planet in my cheek
when I walk away. When I try to find someplace
to go back to.

Told in the first person, the story here is anything but predictable.
A couple out walking encounters a woman reading a poem aloud

"out here in the open". Suddenly the narrator feels the impulse to hug her companion. As she does so a man approaches and asks if can have one, a hug. It is such a simple thing, but how the reader is hooked! Here is reaction to life, absence of anticipation, absence of ideology and posture which frequently attends it. The strength of the first person narrator here is that she is no more important than the other characters in the poem. She is receptive, not programmatic, to the events she is a part of. Even the conclusion, "When I try to find some place / to go back to", is remarkably honest. No one is arbitrarily judged, not the woman reading the poem, not the strange man, not the narrator or her companion. The lives, the reactions, of the characters are respected and honored. The only time that Gallagher succumbs to fashion is here: "Love—that's what they call it." Of course. That's what *everybody* calls it. Why pronounce what is already general knowledge? But this is less than one line in an otherwise marvelous poem. *The Reaper* wishes that Tess Gallagher would, in the future, further develop the narrative gift she has discovered, for "The Hug" is as far from the inheritance of William Cullen Bryant as anything being written today. In the poem the narrative strategy is trusted. That trust produces one of the finest poems Gallagher has ever written. In an age of derivative meditation, narrative will often do that for a poet.

The Dogtown Letters

12 December 1983

Dear Dante,

Yes. You were waiting to hear from another. I decided to write to you instead. I thought it would be better for you, and for me. You know, of course, that you chose Virgil because between you two exists affinity of temperament. As if only he could have led you! A slight, my boy, a slight! A posture, too. All of us are much alike.

We must agree, before we proceed, on essential topics. What *must* we discuss? I have already challenged you on the first point, and I'll come back to that in time. Point two ought to be what separates us. Point three must focus on results (I gave the world you, and everybody else! What did *you* do)—what have writers after us accomplished?

Ah, now. . . Returning to point one. Surely you must confess that we are much alike. My ODYSSEY provides a structure for your COMEDY, for mine was written first in three parts. The first, as you know, portrays Telemachus' hell of uncertainty and self-doubt: *Where* is father? In the second, Odysseus is saved and purges himself of his story. Think of this, dear boy, as Flesh Confession. The third depicts the method he employs to redeem crown, family, home, and revenge, which he exacts and deserves.

Now. What did you do to make this structure your own? How did your strategy differ from mine? Your considerable talent aside, the temperament of your time determined all of your significant alterations. Your monotheistic Christian faith divides us with regard to goals (though your exalted portrayal of Beatrice is, in one sense, a vestige of polytheism). Whereas my lead character struggles to get back to the physical world in which he feels most at home, yours executes a journey (especially Purgatory to Paradise) the result of which is the estranging of humanity from its humanity. You *hate* the body, don't you? Your concern, first and last, is for the soul. The point you hammer home is that it can be saved through reason and through Christ. And that is precisely the paradox that may trip you. I mentioned Beatrice's portrayal as a polytheistic symbol. How so? You elevate her, to my way of thinking, at least to the rank of a minor deity. In moments of crisis your autobiographical traveller turns to her for guidance. Romantic impulses are always primitive in this way; they spring from pre-Christian wells. Imagine what your narrative would have been like had your wanderer gone it alone, stumbling from station to station without the sentiment of Romance.

But you were tugged both ways—on the one hand by belief in your Christian god and on the other by the pagan impulse, which speaks most readily to Man once he assumes the mantle of Guilt. And that is the paradox—your pagan roots ought to lead you to a denial of Christ. Instead, you reject (and so tidily) a romantic for a didactic Christian vision.

I, of course, was up to other things.

29 December 1983

Dear Homer,

The writing of my poem kept me lean, yes. But do I hate the body?

You drank longest and best at the Muse's spring—and I have said so. You drank inspiration like a wine, breathed it in. How can I hate a thing that gives me poetry? All spiritual metaphors are of the body.

And yet, my story is the story of the soul. It extends beyond the body until that day when, made perfect, the body will unite with it.

Your Odysseus loses all companions, all those extensions of his innate power—his men, his ships, his gifts (treasures of sacked, sad, heroic Troy)—and is stripped to his naked wit. Sir, if I have taken my form from your great poem, then notice the seed of faith in your own story. Odysseus is a lonely soul on Calypso's isle, that long wait at the gate to his redemption. Afterwards, step by step, isle by isle, all's restored: Alcinous' gifts replace the lost Trojan treasure; Odysseus claims his crown and wife with sweet revenge, then readies for atonement, for the gift he owes his goddess.

But he is, finally, a wicked man, an evil counsellor, as I have proved. You, sir, are the dim seer, the almost prophet of the true tale. That is, the soul's story. Flesh dims your vision, as eyelids closed against the sun admit only a rose-dim adumbration of the light.

As for structure, certainly I accept the compliment, that skeleton begets skeleton, and that the seat of fire—the heart—of our two works is one throne. Born too early, you could not have known its glory.

The soul extends to every fingertip, to the five senses, and the body's story urges on to be the soul's. It fails so often! Bad poetry. Bad architecture. Corrupt church and city. Poetry, architecture, church and city—all these are innately good. It is the unclean limb that cramps and throws them into Hell.

Finally, Beatrice is no more than what God would wish any of us to be. That's not idolatry, but the soul's perfect extension, the return to its Creator. This story is acted out in the telling, as it was meant to be.

29 December 1983

Dear Dante,

Do I agree with you that the writing of your poem kept you lean? Yes. Wraith-like, maybe. Keep in mind that I am interested, overall, in the consequences of your diet.

You claim that yours is "the story of the soul." Correct. In saying so you imply, at first, that my narrative is unconcerned with the soul. It does not take long, however, for you to contradict yourself by acknowledging "the seed of faith" in my story. Can you have it both ways? I think not. Perfection is the absence of good story; its celebration is (frequently) a dull tale spun for the instruction of half-wits. Perfection, in my mind, is inextricably bound up in an exact, all-encompassing presentation of folly and triumph. If you eviscerate this process, your tale dissolves into lecture. Where is the drama in the story of a character who relentlessly strives to put off the soiled linen of his essential humanity?

The tone of dismissal clouds your justification. Odysseus is, finally, a wicked man, an evil counselor. Praise the Heavens! I will not deny that he is certainly capable of slipping into these robes. But is he finally that? What of Odysseus the good father and noble warrior? What of Odysseus the husband, the lover Penelope awaits? What of their sad, magnificent capacity for forgiveness?

Of course I know that you have long harbored defenses against just this sort of nobility of body and spirit. I note this with tenderness and compassion, my friend. Banished from your Homeland, oppressed by human institutions, what more natural than that you should seek comfort in myth estranged from humanity—humanity which you perceive as a vile adversary. You are, unintentionally, the beginning of the expression of the personal grudge. See what a brood of misshapen followers your monument (a monument to your own denial of humanity) has spawned!

31 December 1983

Dear Homer,

Your flare of temper baffles me, but, I confess, it may be compensation for my condescension. Fair enough. Let's regain the path of our discussion. And I will help this by first making an important concession, and a fine point. Yes, humanity is a soiled thing, not our end, but you must see that its body, all physical corpus, yours and mine, was once a glorious thing. What dragged this precious vessel of the soul down to stinking shit? Humanity—its impulse to veer from the soul's desire for God. Call it the death instinct, but that's another falling away from the true story, a revisionism, rather like your own previsionism. But, again, I condescend.

Tell me, then, what is the story of humanity? I have told you what I believe is the soul's story and you have, harshly, underscored my prejudice. What, if they are truly divergent—and again I concede they are—what is the difference between your human destiny—as you tell it—and my soul's?

Let me make one comment more, since your reference to my "misshapen followers" still stings. How does your epic end? With a battle between Odysseus and the friends of the suitors, suddenly broken off by Athena's intervention. In other words, it ends in mid air. What of the atoning act he was to make, the pilgrimage inland with the oar on his shoulder? It seems to me you start another story, consider it a bad job, and end. Is this not misshapen? You know the symmetry that balances my own poem. Is this symmetry, the order of the stars, not what it seems? I am confused. Elucidate, if you will.

4 January 1984

Dear Dante,

What is the story of humanity? Variety. It is sensation and situation and it *is* our end. The "glorious thing" *is* the body of humanity, not the airy nothing you envision before (and sometimes) after it. The difference between my human destiny and your soul's is this: I strive to lose my identity in the identities of my characters, and they in turn strive for a state of grace *in this life*; you delight in reminding readers that your identity is unquenchable, highly visible, and that you and your cast of characters must suffer through this life (and through much afterlife!) to achieve a state of grace beyond the body. You certainly put the whammy on having a good time!

The difference, my friend, is technique in story telling. My storyteller has overcome personal interest. He has genuinely lost himself in his characters; they take him where they will. You, on the other hand, yank your puppets out of their bodies and yoke them to excruciating labors—punishment for deeds performed here or lesson plans for salvation. The life, the *real* life, falls away. And what is left? A vision of blessed souls whose places, St. Bernard curiously assures you, are assigned by grace, and not according to merit. The separation of merit and grace is one of countless instances where you take your narrative out of the hands of men. You become dangerously mystical, which I abhor. My gods may intervene, decree, destroy, but they do so like men and women. They have been invested with something your god lacks—humanity, which is fallibility. Both of us are merciless in our pursuit of truth; because I told the truth of body *and* spirit, you were able to indulge your prejudice and concentrate only on the latter. You succeeded in producing a magnificent Half-Truth.

Finally, I wish to dress your wound after removing the sting of an earlier comment. When I referred to your "misshapen followers," I did not do so to injure *you*. Surely we are capable of commenting on those choking strategies that followed us. You take me to task for faulty symmetry in the conclusion of my story. I did not grow weary of the tale I had to tell. I told it. The act of atonement is suggested, the continuing narrative implied (for all good epics could go on forever). But after the suitors are killed, I had concluded the essential narrative I had to tell. You might liken my ending to a coda, much like the prayer you offer up to your god for the ability to render some glimpse of celestial glory in your writing. Or perhaps I was attempting to mollify the gods I had harnessed so effectively to this earth.

In closing, my dear fellow, I must warn you against "the order of the stars." Discoveries are daily made that suggest what we thought we knew of illumination above is actually illusion. A crumbling anchor? I would like you to examine this structure, then bring it down to earth by answering the charge that you are so at home, or seem to be, in Hell. And are you "most humane" (as many have said) in Purgatory?

15 January 1984

Dear Homer,

You have "told the truth of the body *and* the spirit"? Hardly. That the body has a certain stamina that might be called spirit, you acknowledge through Odysseus' heroism and, at times, his self-preserving, wily cowardice. But that I have told a "Half-Truth," however magnificent you acknowledge it to be, is, of course, completely incomprehensible to me.

But let us speak of variety, since it is your first point that the story of humanity is such, and it is one with which I agree. If fact, you do not deny anywhere in making your point than my story lacks variety.

Nothing is so various as the light of paradise.

But mine is a vertical, yours a horizontal variety. At the very bottom of the pit is the most bestial of creation, mere hungry flesh that thrives on its own indulgence. Your own Odysseus met such beasts. The man-devourers who plucked his crew and ate them. Surely these examples of variety are not glorious things, except as adversaries. Surely, when having behaved swinishly, his men were turned by Circe *into* swine, Odysseus did not applaud this manifestation of man's animal flesh. As the steps of hell descend, the flesh grows heavier, grosser. Look at the suitors stuffing themselves. They sink with full stomachs into Hades.

And in Hades we find the place your imagination balks. You speak of the truth of the human spirit, yet look at your conception of the afterlife. No glory but penalty for all: Achilles sullen beside the fallen suitors. There's your horizontality: a brief space of glorious life, various life, and then a monotonous eternity. Why?

Nothing is so various as eternity.

Two points more, one in which you baffle me, the other with which I agree.

At home in Hell? Please, look again. I feel a fellowship with those I loved in life or knew of in life: Paolo and Francesca, ny teacher Ser Brunetto, and even Ugolino, horrid in the ice. Their stories, when they were in the world and not yet fallen, strike my heart, and these I let them tell. But I am not at home with them in their eternity.

But yes, of course, in Purgatory humanity is my theme. Humanity as it is perfected, as it will be perfected in the end. Again. I must claim some variety for myself here. What is more various than my mountain with its seashore, valleys, colored stairs and friezes, its winding path and garden at the top?

Finally, let us admit the difference between our epics. It seems so clear and yet we've said nothing of it. Life is horizontal, and this is your theme. But the afterlife is my discovery (although Odysseus saw my mountain), and it is vertical.

21 January 1984

Dear Dante,

Nothing is so various as any good story told well. What does the mesmerized audience care if a tale is illuminated by the light of Paradise or the spark of original utterance? They will honor you as long as they perceive reflections of themselves in your drama.

I readily accept your horizontal-vertical definition, but let us agree further on its implication. I agree if by *horizontal* you mean lakes, oceans, the roundness of the earth, the space inside an embrace, that same space which connects body and spirit; I agree if by *vertical* you mean the waterfall (which seeks completion in a pool), the geyser, the drill, the man, woman, and child erect and at odds with a horizontal universe. These are the implications of your definition, and they describe the differences in our methods perfectly.

From this pinnacle of agreement, we ought to be concerned with the consequences of our methods—and I know we are concerned. Your vertical reality is inclined toward psychological case studies, which your journeyman imitators have indulged in for centuries. They lack your Divine Art and pester audiences with drab insights and crabbed confessions drained of dramatic sparkle. Your own masterpiece provided a landscape they could not wait to colonize.

And how is this possible? My friend, Hades is not the "place my imagination balks." Rather, your conduct there provides an open book of your fears, your political trials and exile. Consider the movement of your first 34 Cantos. At Acheron you fall into a trance and are roused by a clap of thunder. Your god admonishes and prods you with this "reminder." It is not surprising that you meet me there, for you fear damnation and the possibility that your talent might not be up to the task you have set it. Significantly, it is the in fourth circle that your narrative slows down, for it is here that you begin to face your political failures and taste the bitterness of your exile. In your seventh and eighth circles, you dwell long on the violent punishments perpetrated there. Is this not wish fulfillment? It is far from coincidental that in your sixteenth canto you meet the spirits of three military men who are, in fact, your countrymen. The symbol they provide prepares you for the lingering journey through the ten gulfs of your eighth circle, the terrible journey which confronts your own sense of isolation and frustration in this life.

Yes, this is your vertical strategy, a distillation of one strategy I employed and yoked to others. My tradition was larger than yours, which allowed for greater variety. Of course, you compensate with grand intensity—a quality many of your followers lack.

29 January 1984

Homer, Sir:

My journeymen imitators. My misshapen followers. Lacking and self-indulgent. You have harped on this theme almost from the beginning and I have had enough.

Who are they? Not a single name do you produce.

But I will describe them generally, too, for if their insights are drab and their confessions drained of sparkle (an oddly mixed metaphor), they still, as I perceive them, WRITE.

And your descendants? Certainly the few novelists have turned to historical potboilers, the poets are long dead, and yet, I know where to find your progeny. For your time has come again, oral and preliterate. Your poems were receptacles of what a culture was, archives indeed, and your sons and daughters sang them to the ears of illiterate kings. Who are your descendants? The creatures on the television screen that tell in their multitudinous monotony their nearly illiterate listeners what they are or should be or will be, if they follow the practices performed.

You tradition was larger when it included me, but now we know it was mine that included yours. Now your tradition continues to extend but not to keep its center, like an empire whose outskirts thrive while the far away capital has fallen. And those outskirts! How alien they would seem to the seat of the culture, to the emperor himself.

Poetry is in bad shape, yes, and I will shoulder one stone of the blame, if I must; I am not proud of it. For what I wrote was a metaphor for reality, The Reality. Now I am read for my virtuosity as a poet. Here, I am master of the plain style. There, I am master of metaphor. Here, I am politically engaged. There, I am a narrative poet. In a word, I am merely words, disintegrated, bricks broken from the edifice, stones.

And you—you are no better. So, let us cease this baiting and carping about what each of us has wrought, totally involuntarily, since we are dead, and our works are merely starlight.

God forgive me for my flare of temper. You, too.

2 February 1984

Dante, My Son,

Your letter warmed me! Such feverish outbursts, from you, are good—for you. It is not unlike a voice I entertained and implanted once in Telemachus; I discarded those drafts because my story did not call for a son strong in his anger—it made me make him so desperate in his impotence. I wonder if you ever identified with him; I suspect you did. Being dead, I know it.

But I digress, and lest I wax morbid allow me to break with your habit of avoiding direct questions. "Who are they?" you cry—your "misshapen followers." I am staggered and amused by your exasperation. Gaze again on your 17th hellish canto; experience again its deadly sting. For that matter, journey further into the succeeding circle and reacquaint yourself with the flatterers. Your self-serving progeny, or representation of them, are scattered throughout your system. Yes, you knew them all too well. None of them (to honor who is among us) "will dine at journey's end with Landor and with Donne."

Sweet Coz, what would be served by naming them? Would their names not turn to hideous sores on your tongue? Mine festers if I even think of such utterance! We know who they are, and so do they (spanning the ages like billboards). Is that not enough? Your anger unwittingly defends them—defense by implication—and I know that is not your intention. "Your tradition was larger when it included me, but now we know it was mine that included yours."

What do you mean by this flagrant inaccurate declaration? Note the contemporary ring to your sentence. If I did not know you better, I would perceive that you were low on salt! And your television analogy? Hysterical projection. It is your face in the mirror, not mine. But it is not really your face, either; it is the image of your face created by so many wayward, modern enthusiasts. They cannot shed the habit of dwelling on the way they consume their daily bread. Let us leave them, blabbering beefcakes showered with prizes, and revel in deathless death. Let us tell stories to one another; let us honor the true sons who will come. As for your outburst, allow me to paraphrase one of your favorite characters: "Forgive him, for he knows not what he does."

5 February 1984

Dear Homer,

The story of every man and woman is the story of their souls, the simple souls that issue from God's hand.

These stories occur on earth: hedged round, fenced in, paved and routed, mapped and charted, confined and glorified there, as the soul is in the flesh.

These stories interest us because our bodies do, the earth does. And your body more than mine, your soul, your fate on earth and in heaven, more than mine, interest me.

This interest in the other is a tenet of my faith—as poet, which I believe is orthodox with my faith as man. As soul.

I want to know the stories of my friends and enemies, their ends on earth and their translation into the world beyond. And I believe they, too, having been curious in this way, want others to know. Only the humiliated of greatest degradation want to be forgotten. Only the exalted at the most high are indifferent. And yet, their extremity is telling.

What is the news? What happened to him, to her, to them? My poem tells you.

I assume the interest in the other which is a seed of love. Only a poet of this time would say that to ask the hard question is simple: How are you? How do you do? We do want to the know the answers to these, long as they may take, difficult as they may be to answer.

It is thus I will claim my monstrous brood of descendants. This curiosity, turned inward, divides each from each.

The interest in oneself becomes self-interest. Without a daily awareness of the other there is no eternal acknowledgement. No gratitude for creation. No soul that links to God and others. No interest in their histories, their stories.

Today, poetry is self-absorption, which is tantamount to self-annihilation. Euclid tells us that between one point and another is an infinite series of points. Islands, if you will. Levels. A distance to travel, nevertheless. Ah, but to the self-absorbed, infinity is futility, the eternal terminates.

And so, without love for the other, without the line to the other, without the narrative that draws that line, without the story—there is no poetry as I know it. Or as you know it.

Perhaps, I have stretched Euclid's point.

But my God is a geometer, as yours is a magician. Both seek the most direct route between two points *that will give a story*. Indeed, I am being sly. And yet I swear I am sincere about the number: two points, at least. I and the other make a story. The poem is the record of the journey. It is written for others.

14 February 1984

Dear Dante,

All you have written your last epistle is true. Our differences evaporate like the exhaustion of Odysseus on Alcinous' shore. Two Points—yes. And the line that connects them. And essential love that envelops the telling.

How does one *learn* such love? How doe one *achieve* it? By focus, by fluid adjustment of the lens that is the eye, encompassing wide angle and close shot; by comprehending the intangibles—intelligence and heart (animals are innately more capable of this than man); by living in a condition of permanent erosion (the barriers surrounding selfhood wash away); by blunting our axes until only the implements of gathering remain. Then, and only then, are we worthy of The Harvest.

The stories of such travelers, great and small, endure and are endearing. They make insignificant all argument.

I justifiably claim for myself an addiction to selflessness. In this condition I know that one accepts the idea of vertical only within the context of *human* achievement as degradation. The horizontal is *history* in which all humanity lives. Man is responsible to no inhuman standard by which to measure himself; to believe otherwise is to prefer illusion over reality, to strip the story from its form.

Narrative conveys the story into the light of comprehension. Poets who know this need not seek eternity; it will find them.

How to Write Narrative Poetry
A Reaper Checklist

1. *A beginning, a middle, and an end*

Just as it is hard to get the whole story, it is hard to allow a story to tell itself. Poets become enamored of a segment, an anecdote, and are content with nothing more. When this occurs, like the detached tail of a lizard, the story just wriggles and dies.

2. *Observation*

The poet whose senses are attuned to all of the elements of the story can create the impression of participation. In a good narrative poem the narrator is a witness.

3. *Compression of time*

Whether a narrative poem is 4600 or 46 lines long, the poet must handle the passage of time in far less space than prose would require. This restriction demands the poet's restraint in choice of language. A rhythm is necessary, too, one that arises out of the story. No matter how the poet captures it, in meter or typography, rhythm is movement, movement is time, and time must be compressed.

4. Containment

No character and no action may violate the essence of that character or act. A character must be consistent; an act must logically follow acts preceding it. Even illogical acts must be logically constructed.

5. Illumination of private gestures

A character's gestures define that character. They also bind that character to other characters. A poet who makes a character's private gestures accessible is engaged in the act of definition not by proclamation but by presentation.

6. Understatement

This device sustains and contributes to the development of drama. Without drama there is no tension; without tension the story sags.

7. Humor

Humor is an exploitation of intimacy. The most frequent form of this, in poetry anyway, is irony. But humor in a narrative poem might display more tenderness than irony allows. Humor may also change the pace subtly, allowing the reader to reflect on what has been read and prepare for what is to come.

8. Location

Memorable literature is the history of authors who have successfully presented their intimate involvement with an identifiable region.

9. Memorable characters

Any character is potentially memorable. One might tell us something about ourselves we did not know (or own up to) before we met him or her. But our fascination with character is also a desire to connect with someone who is not ourselves, not even like us, as far as we can tell. Obviously, we have always read stories in order to find out what happens to others and to see how they act and why.

10. A compelling subject

The way any story is told will determine whether or not it is compelling to readers that know how to read narrative in poems. Subjects resist authors lacking the experience, knowledge, and staying power to tell them. This alone explains the inability of many poets to write narrative. It also explains their reluctance to try, their fear of the form, and their fearful denigration of it.

The Reaper will now employ his own checklist and examine poems. The first poem, "The Gleaning" by Jared Carter, appeared in *The Reaper* #9; the second poem, "Painters of Angels and Seraphim" by Charles Simic, appeared in *The Missouri Review* (Volume VII, Number 3). The first poem is an example of flawless narrative. The second is not.

The Gleaning

All day long they have been threshing
And something breaks: the canvas belt
That drives the separator flies off,
Parts explode through the swirl
Of smoke and chaff, and he is dead
Where he stands—drops the pitchfork
As they turn to look at him—and falls.
They carry him to the house and go on

With the work. Five wagons and their teams
Stand waiting, it is still daylight,
There will be time enough for grieving.

When the undertaker comes from town
He brings the barber, who must wait
Till the women finish washing the body.
Neighbors arrive from the next farm
To take the children. The machines
Shut down, one by one, horses
Are led away, the air grows still
And empty, then begins to fill up
With the sounds of cicada and mourning dove.
The men stand along the porch, talking
In low voices, smoking their cigarettes;
The undertaker sits in the kitchen
With the family.
                    In the parlor
The barber throws back the curtains
And talks to this man, whom he has known
All his life, since they were boys
Together. As he works up a lather
And brushes it onto his cheeks,
He tells him the latest joke. He strops
The razor, tests it against his thumb,
And scolds him for not being more careful.
Then with darkness coming over the room
He lights a lamp, and begins to scrape
At the curve of the throat, tilting the head
This way and that, stretching the skin,
Flinging the soap into a basin, gradually
Leaving the face glistening and smooth.

And as though his friend had fallen asleep
And it were time now for him to stand up

And stretch his arms, and look at his face
In the mirror, and feel the closeness
Of the shave, and marvel at his dreaming —
The barber trims the lamp, and leans down,
And says, for the last time, his name.

1. A beginning, a middle, and an end

Carter constructs this poem in three parts: the man's death, the
general response to that event, and the barber's specific reaction to
it. Other poets might have been satisfied with the man's death or the
barber's behavior as subjects. The story would be diminished, be-
coming merely anecdotal. Carter patiently makes a story of many
layers as complex and as simple as life itself.

2. Observation

Carter's narrator observes everything that is critical to the story
he is telling. When the accident occurs that leads to the man's death,
the narrator sees him fall as the other workers "turn to look at him."
In the second stanza the narrator watches the women washing the
body, the neighbors arriving from the next farm to the take the chil-
dren, the machines shut down, horses led away, the air growing still
and empty then filling up with sounds of cicadas and mourning
doves, men standing (not sitting) along the porch, talking (in low
voices), smoking cigarettes, the undertaker in the kitchen with the
family—and then the barber. Everything and everyone relevant to
the story. Not one observation is excessive. And the narrator speaks
with the authority of a witness.

3. Compression of time

The Reaper conservatively estimates that six to eight hours elapse
in "The Gleaning." The careful reader emerges from the poem feel-

ing as if he has witnessed *everything* that took place in that period. Never does he suffer the sting of authorial intrusion, of language aimed to interfere. Contributing to this compression is a subtle but powerful rhythm created by long, accumulating sentences emphasizing verbs and, culminating in the final stanza, conjunctions. Carter's story is told in 46 lines. An accomplished prose writer might require 46 pages.

4. Containment

The barber, once he commences shaving the dead man (who was his friend), performs as he always has when practicing his trade.

5. Illumination of private gestures

The Reaper calls attention to the poem's concluding lines: "The barber trims the lamp, and leans down. / And says, for a last time, his name." The symbolic trimming of the lamp and the barber speaking his friend's name affirm what we have imagined about the relationship between the two men. They also tell us about the barber, his practicality, loyalty, compassion, and sadness.

6. Understatement

Consider the last line of the first stanza: "There will be time enough for grieving." A man has just died, suddenly and horribly. The line itself is simply stated, but it contains an emphatic promise (there *will* be time . . .) that makes us dread and anticipate the grief to come. It is odd that the narrator should say this, but it is truth itself.

7. Humor

The barber tells the dead man the latest joke. He also scolds him for not being more careful. These moments evoke Lord Byron's prescription for sorrow: "I will laugh so that I will not weep." They also change the pace of the poem, allow the reader a momentary pause before the next surge forward.

8. Location

"The Gleaning" is a portrait of rural (which is to say most of) America, and within the context of Carter's work, of Indiana. The art of the poem is in giving a first-hand account of what must be a story from an earlier time. Such immediacy is possible only from a poet, like Carter, who is immersed in his region.

9. Memorable characters

All of the characters, even the supporting characters, are memorable in "The Gleaning." All of them are attached to specific, vivid tasks without which the action of the poem would disintegrate. The women *wash* the dead body, the neighbors arrive to *take the children*, the men, sad and frustrated, *stand* along the porch, the undertakers *sits*, but he does so in the kitchen, sharing the family's grief. Nature plays a part, too, but one carefully created by the poet, so that as the human activity ends, the waning day is left naturally to cicada and mourning dove; knowing nothing of grief, their voices make it keener. The barber becomes memorable as we witness his fluctuation back and forth between pragmatic professional and devastated friend. Finally, the dead man is made memorable not by the fact and dramatic circumstances of his death, but by the chain of events it creates. All of these characters tell us more than we might have known about death and its aftermath and about friendship.

10. A Compelling Subject

"The Gleaning" tells the story of a farm worker who is killed by an equipment malfunction. He is taken back to the house and prepared for burial. *The Reaper*'s last two sentences are examples of reportage. "The Gleaning" is an example of narrative poetry which tells the story of the friendship between two men, one living and one dead. It also tells the story of death and of how one community responds to it.

Now, *The Reaper* turns to Charles Simic's poem.

Painters of Angels and Seraphim

> After a long lunch of roast lamb
> And many glasses of heavy red wine,
> I fell asleep in a rowboat
> That I never got around to untie
> From its mooring under the willows
> That went on fussing over my head
> As if to make the shade even deeper.
>
> I woke once to pull my shirt off,
> And once when I heard my name
> Called by a woman, distant and worried,
> Since it was past sundown
> The water reflecting the dark hills,
> And the sky of that chilly blue
> That used to signify a state of grace.

1. A beginning, a middle, and an end

The entire poem could be a beginning, a middle, or an end to some longer narrative, but it certainly does not comprise all three elements within itself. Nevertheless, its narrative form hints that it is one of the three deliberately cut free from the story and meant to be complete in itself—which it is not.

2. Observation

Perhaps, the speaker is too sleepy to observe much. The most sympathetic reading discovers three details of interest: the "fussing" of the willows, the calling woman, and the color of the sky after sundown. But since they neither lead to nor contribute to a story, they are merely atmospheric, and observation serves only itself.

3. Compression of time

Time certainly is compressed here, but how skillfully is its passage evoked? The speaker falls asleep and awakes twice, once to make himself more comfortable and once more when he hears his name called (presumably he does go back to sleep the second time). Meanwhile, the narrative of these events creates a rhythm that ends in stasis, a nostalgic "used to be" before nodding off.

4. Containment

What is the unifying logic of this? Satiety? Sluggishness? Yes, those must be the reasons he is too full and tired to respond to anything.

5. Illumination of private gestures

Now, this is one element that is certainly present, and because there are so few others, it makes this poem all the more frustrating as a failed narrative. Our speaker enjoys napping in a rowboat; waking he pulls off his shirt, possibly to help him go back to sleep (it must be a warm day); waking again, he has heard a woman call his name but instead of answering he makes a most remarkable observation about the sky. Of course, without the whole story, one inference is as good as another. *The Reaper* sees a drowsy hedonism in which the speaker detects a vestige of (his own?) "chilly blue" religious austerity.

6. *Understatement*

Without drama there can be no understatement. The last line apparently is meant as an understatement, since "used to signify" undercuts the loftier "state of grace." All *The Reaper* hears, though, is the winding down of a record turned off too soon.

7. *Humor*

Simic's inimitable sense of humor is not present here. It is very clear that narrative has become an alien form to him. In another poem of his, the jokes would have begun with line one.

8. *Location*

Who knows where we are?

9. *Memorable characters*

Besides the speaker, who really does nothing memorable except choose a rowboat for a bed, there is only the distant, worried woman. It is too bad that we never meet her. But then we are not meant to meet her, and this is also unfortunate.

10. *A compelling subject*

Simic never discovers it, although he seems to be on his way. In an interview that appears with this poem in the same issue of *The Missouri Review*, the following exchange occurs which, naturally, caught *The Reaper's* attention.

Interviewer: Your work has always stood somewhere outside the narrative mode, but do you ever find yourself drifting in that direction?

Simic: I hope not. Most of the so-called narrative poems just plod. They have no sense of the line, nor do they imagine well. When poets forget what imagination can do they get into these linear, prosy, redundant, long-winded poems. It's impossible to tell a story, the whole story, in twenty lines. The art consists of making a few details and images say everything. They should study Strand's "The Untelling." There's a masterpiece for you.

Interviewer: But don't most poems of any kind just plod? I was really wondering about the exceptional few. Or are you saying that at some point the imagination and the narrative are antithetical?

Simic: No. Imagination and narrative go fine together. Consider myths, fairy tales, prose poems, etc. However, most narrative poems I see operate largely in the framework of realism.

Interviewer: I notice reading reviews of your books that critics at times have a tendency to read your poems as parables. Is that the result of your working beyond the framework of realism?

Simic: I don't know. I don't write parables. If I say "rats in diapers" that's to be taken literally.

If Simic believes it's not possible to tell the whole story in twenty lines, would he have needed only six more to complete it in "Painter of Angels and Seraphim"? What of his reference to Strand's long, inverted narrative, which *The Reaper* agrees is a masterpiece? Is Simic being sarcastic? As for realism, Simic's poem seems as realistic as

Carter's, but realism is not why it fails. Finally, Simic's claim that he does not write parables is simply unbelievable. The last collection of his which contained anything like short, successful narrative poems, of the sort he does commend, was *Charon's Cosmology* (1977). In that book he showed that his kind of story can be told in twenty lines or less. Otherwise, twenty lines is an arbitrary limit that Jared Carter's "The Gleaning" explodes.

Forever Young
A Survey, conducted by The Reaper

In *The Reaper #11* and *The Reaper #12*, he announced his intention to scrutinize the two latest Dagwood Sandwich Anthologies: NEW AMERICAN POETS OF THE '80's, edited by Jack Myers and Roger Weingarten (Wampeter Press), and THE MORROW ANTHOLOGY OF YOUNGER AMERICAN POETS, edited by Dave Smith and David Bottoms, with an introduction by Anthony Hecht (Quill). considering the odd delay, *Reaper* readers deserve an explanation.

The *volume* of work was considerable. When *The Reaper's* first announcement appeared under "Coming Attractions" in #11, he had only begun to walk the halls of what he calls The Conception-and-Delivery Room in our heads. Altogether, there were 169 poets whose work demanded probing, punishment, or praise. Appropriately, *The Reaper* went everywhere and did everything with the anthologies. His arms grew big with constant referral. Always an admirer of strength, if not weight, *The Reaper* made love to these muscular publications. He courted them, married them, quarreled with them, and moved out. He came back, too. He came back because he believes in The On-Going Dialogue; he came back because the books themselves, chubby, legless tree shrouds, could not come after him.

Then, one night on a walk through the cemetery, *The Reaper* began to ask questions of the stones. "What, Josiah Elder, Born 1853—died 1896, would you say about the poems of Robert Pinsky? And what would you, Hettie Dubonnet born 1868—died 1931, say to the work of Herbert Scott?" *The Reaper* smiled, not at his own folly in seeking opinions of The Dead, but at his slow wit. It came to him like death that if he were to offer insightful commentary he must seek the opinions of those who matter most: The Readers.

Thus *The Reaper* devised the following plan. He would compile a list of Readers who did not have any immediate stake in the reception of the anthologies. They would not be chairpeople of English or Writing Departments with jobs to fill or readings and workshops to offer; they would not be professional or personal friends of the contributors. Just fair Readers. *The Reaper* would send them copies of the anthologies with a general list of questions. Readers would be free to respond as they saw fit, neither restricted by length nor conflicts with editorial opinion.

The Reaper considered his plan and saw that it was good. The following letters are representative responses chosen from many *The Reaper* received. *The Reaper* wishes to thank all those Readers who responded for sharing their valuable opinions with our audience.

Lynn Cannella, PhD.
New York City

Dear Reaper,

My work as a clinical psychologist does not necessarily qualify me as a semiotician, but your questions about the appearance or packaging of the two poetry anthologies you have sent incline me to believe you would like the books analyzed as "signs." After some thought about your questions and after looking the two editions over, I think I can offer some interpretive speculations that might seem useful, even though their accuracy could be doubtful. The behavior of the group, in this case poets, anthologists, and publishers of anthologies, can only be interpreted correctly if it corresponds at important points to the behavior of the examiner and her own group. The notion that a Martian can give us insights into ourselves is true only if in some way we behave like Martians. *The Morrow Anthology of Younger American Poets* and *New American Poets of the '80s* may or may not be understandable to one who does not consider herself professionally linked to them, but as the writing of poetry is a human activity and the production and marketing of books is, too, along with the reading of them, I will do my best to write my Persian letter.

Both anthologies are cumbersome oversized paperbacks. They weigh nearly the same, although the Morrow includes some 39 more poets, longer introductions, and photographs of the poets. Usually the weightiness of a tome signifies its importance. However, anthologies, like dictionaries, must be inclusive and give the sense that all one wants is within the covers. The Morrow anthology costs $17.95. Its weight suggests that one will get one's money's worth. The other, published by Wampeter Press, cost $9.95. One might feel, hefting it in the hand, that one is getting a bargain.

The contrast in cover designs is remarkable. Part of the Morrow's title is printed on what appear to be the lines of grade school writing paper, those widely spaced bars that allow for the simple task of learning to write. These younger poets, after all, are learning their craft. Yet the lettering of the word "Poets" in the title is one-third the size of the cover and printed in aqua-pastels. This along with some other subtle touches like the diamond decorations, the use of the ampersand, the insignia of the Morrow "Quill" book all imply expertise. Rather than a primer's lines we begin to see the skeleton of the layout. This design then is high tech, as contemporary as skindiving. On the back of the book are a paragraph by the publisher, an excerpt from the editor's preface, and an excerpt from the introduction by Anthony Hecht, an older poet. This is a surfeit of prose, as we are used to see in advertisements for certain low tar and nicotine cigarettes. Prose is the medium of truth and advertises professionalism and believability.

The cover of the Wampeter anthology is a glossy gray barred diagonally with slashes of neon pink. This combination of gray and red, specifically, can be detected on nearly every businessman and official in the U.S. today. They are the power colors of the 1980's, and appear most often as a gray suit and a red tie. (The red tie has lately been replaced by a yellow tie, but the message is the same. These are the colors of the bruised survivor. He or she can take it and dish it out.) Like the title of the Morrow, the Wampeter's is in black letters. The Wampeter's letters have serifs, whereas the Morrow's are sans serif. There is a suggestion—and it may only be a suggestion—of the conservative in the Wampeter anthology's cover. This is consistent with much that we see today associated with youth. Flashy but not nihilistic. Many poets appear in both anthologies and a glance through at their poems (and their pictures) discovers no revolutionaries or anarchists. On the back of the Wampeter are the names of all the poets. looking within I see that the introduction itself by editors Jack Myers and Roger Weingarten would have fit on the back of the Morrow anthology. Modesty is clearly the message of such brevity—or very great arrogance. We humbly (or haughtily) present the best we know of. It may be pointed out here that the best in both books includes the anthologists themselves. This seems to me a perfectly acceptable mode of behavior, and no more narcissistic than agreeing to be included in an anthology in the first place. If all are poets, and all are young, then by all means all should be included. I note only that the design of pink slashes cuts through the double column of names on the back of the Wampeter and at the bottom of the back cover is an elaborate, vaguely Aztec design surrounding a big W above script reading "a George Murphy book" (all of this in neon pink, too). This, along with the odd name of the publisher, suggests a personal touch, that of the independent press, and a friendly narcissism, too. That the slashes quadrisect the names of the poets is faintly disturbing. If Mr. Murphy is a poet himself, then his work is absent, yet his name is present. This appears to be an inscrutable point that I will have to demur from, as an alien.

I suppose the biggest apparent difference between the two an-
thologies that might amount to some psychological manifestation is
the presence of photographs in one and not in the other. The
Morrow anthology includes photographs of the poets; the Wampeter
does not. Although actual production values seem to be roughly
equivalent (the Wampeter is sewn and glued, however; while the
Morrow is perfectbound, a cheaper process, I understand), surely it
costs more money to print pictures. Does the Wampeter suffer by
comparison since it lacks photographs? I am afraid so. We like look-
ing at photographs of other people when we are also looking at ev-
idence of their work. Reading of the murderer's crimes, we want to
see his picture. The image is ingrained in much that we appreciate,
at least where words are concerned, in religion, in art—all this is
quite well known. In any event, it seems to me, as a rank outsider,
that the photographs in the Morrow must be of most interest to the
group itself. Many of them are mere snapshots, all of them seem
posed, none is candid, and their quality varies. None of the por-
traits strikes a responsive chord like the bust of Shakespeare or
Beethoven or a photograph of the young James Joyce or one of the
fortyish George Eliot. In other words, I didn't recognize anybody,
and my appreciation, as far as I could tell, was not exactly deepened
by seeing the man or the woman behind the poems. I was struck by
the variety, from the slick professional glamour of some, to the odd
inclinations of head and obscuring props of others, to the near can-
did quality of a very few. Again, the manifestation bespoke merely
a harmless narcissism, as does so much here. Why include pho-
tographs at all then? The general reader must require them, as he or
she requires images with all he or she digests. And the professional
reader wants to see what poet X, Y, or Z really looks like.

That there are no photographs in the Wampeter does not seem
to be the statement that their presence is in the Morrow. I did, how-
ever, detect that on average there were about the same number of
poems per poet in the Wampeter, whereas the number varied be-
tween four and eight in the Morrow. Editor Dave Smith is repre-

sented by eight poems in the Morrow. And editor David Bottoms is represented by six poems. This makes a kind of sense since Smith appears to be the senior editor. Yet no one in their age group exceeds their own number of poems and some have fewer. Naturally, Smith and Bottoms would be aware of their own best work. And, again, the acceptable narcissism of this cannot be a pathology if the group admits it, as it clearly does in such a poetry anthology. Otherwise, the anthologists would have had to exclude themselves altogether or represent their work only nominally.

Let me end with a few remarks on this, finally, very interesting note. Both volumes are really manifestations of their compilers, the editors themselves. Smith and Bottoms have set a clear cut-off of 1940 for the birthdate of the young poets to be included in their anthology. Bottoms is still under forty; it appears that those poets near his age could actually be called young. Smith is over forty and so are a number of other poets in the anthology. If a cutoff date of 1945 had been made, thus including only poets under forty, Smith would have had to suppress a legitimate desire to be included in his own anthology.

There is no such guideline announced by Myers and Weingarten and it is harder to infer a motive in their choices, especially when they include poets in their 50's. Theirs is an anthology of "new" poets, although on the back cover the poets are called "best" and "younger." The point seems to be that here, as everywhere, the boundary of youth is being extended, because Americans are growing older. This seems to be an altogether healthy phenomenon, for the present, but will have to be adjusted at some future date in response to the emergence of a genuinely younger generation.

To end where I began, these are big books. Had each anthology printed work only by those poets it included under the age of forty, the Morrow book would have been reduced by 37 poets and the Wampeter by 24. This is over a one-third reduction for each book. Then, they would have weighed a little bit less but, perhaps, would have more accurately represented what they advertised. On the other hand, the group for which these books were made clearly has its own definition of youth. And that is quite all right, as I have said. At least for now.

Hubert Jeffries
Attorney-at-Law
Tempe, AZ.

Dear Reaper:

I received the two anthologies of poetry and your amusing query. Though I am certainly no expert, I consider myself an intelligent, above average reader, and I am delighted to respond to the works in question.

To begin with, I had no idea that contemporary poetry was so healthy. I assume that as in other market endeavors in which production, packaging, and distribution are indications of health, an important indication of poetry's health is its publication. Good for the poets!

I was intrigued, generally, by the present work. Most of the poets were new to me, my reading outside the demands of my own profession seldom extending beyond novels, literature on conservation, animal rights, flying, and an occasional copy of *The New Yorker*. Thanks to the latter, I had heard of a few of these poets—but only a few. However, this is inconsequential to the questions at hand.

Specifically, *why* was I intrigued? I pondered this self-directed query for some time. On the surface, an immediate answer presented itself: I was intrigued because I was curious. I have mentioned my passion for reading and the restraint that the practice of my profession has unfortunately imposed on it. Because you were so thoughtful in sending me the material, I resolved that I would make time in which to consider it. The more I read, the more my curiosity sustained me. It sustained me to the extent that, after several days, I began to feel that I was often reading work I would never return to again. This revelation encourage me to consider additional factors contributing to my sense of intrigue. I began to realize that, in addition to a novice's curiosity, I was intrigued to a deeper level by what I was *not* getting out of the material.

Fearing that fatigue might encourage me to shortchange many poems, I put aside the anthologies and read, in rare, free hours, Frost, Whitman, and Tolstoy's *Anna Karenina*. You might compare my strategy to that of a diner clearing his palate with a cool sherbet between bottles of wine. And when I returned to the anthologies I discovered what, for me, was missing.

The editors of both anthologies, faced with a harrowing task, failed to devise a compelling argument for their own selection process and the chosen material. Having written, and read, countless legal briefs and opinions, I am convinced of the necessity for clear, convincing argument. Without standards (and standards based solely on intuition will not do), without formidable belief in a Scheme of Things, in a driving, underlying mechanism, an argument and its conclusions will not survive. The editors, for whatever reasons, lack the ability to argue convincingly, and their anthologies suffer for it.

In addition, many of the poets seemed to leave too much out of their poems. Like any good reader, I am most attracted to a good story told well. It must delight me, hold my interest, and inspire me to look at what I did not know or look again at what I thought I knew.

In the Morrow anthology, I found twenty poems that accomplished this. They are "Almost Grown" by Ai, "The Desk" by David Bottoms, "Big Sheep Knocks You about" by Sharon Bryan, "Dusting" by Rita Dove, "Elizabeth's War With the Christmas Bear" by Norman Dubie, "Mannequins" by Daniel Mark Epstein, "Black Silk" (also in Wampeter) by Tess Gallagher, "Yellow Light" by Garrett Kaoru Hongo, "The Sergeant: by Don Johnson, "Coon Hunt, Sixth Month (1955)" by Sydney Lea, "Sex Without Love" and "The One Girl at the Boy's Party" by Sharon Olds, "Sharks, Caloosahatchee River" by Greg Pape, "The Purpose of Altar Boys" (also in Wampeter) by Alberto Rios, "The Roundhouse Voices" by Dave Smith, "Shoplifters" by Maura Stanton, "Land of Little Sticks, 1945" and "Sloops in the Bay" by James Tate, "Women's Locker Room" by Marilyn Waniek, and "Singles" (also in Wampeter) by Michael Waters.

In the Wampeter anthology I discovered sixteen poems—beside the three cited in Morrow as well—I will read again and again. They are "Bleeder" and "Black Dog, Red Dog" by Stephen Dobyns, "Parsley" by Rita Dove, "The Hug" by Tess Gallagher," "Movie Within a Movie" by Denis Johnson, "Burning Out" by Robert Long, "The Oven Loves the TV Set" by Heather McHugh, "A Story" by Susan Mitchell, "Put Your Mother on the Ceiling" by Greg Pape, "History of My Heart" (though some of it does seem to be overwritten) by Robert Pinsky, "Providence" by David St. John, "Spit" and "Tar" by C. K. Williams, and "Under the Sign of Cancer" by Carolyne Wright.

Now all that remains is for me to share a few observations as to why the other poets and their poems failed to survive, for me, beyond the satisfaction of my curiosity. I have already stated what I look for as a reader. Therefore, it ought to be clear that the poets I left off my list did not satisfy my hopes. They did not satisfy me because in their attempts to invite me into their worlds, they simply cut me off. Most of the time, this seemed to occur just as the act of telling a story became reflexive. In other words, at key moments, fledgling stories with grand potential veered off-course, becoming stories *about* the act of telling stories. It was almost as if the storyteller lost faith in the story, or in its characters. At times, I was reminded of well-coached witnesses who nevertheless begin to disintegrate under the pressure of persistent cross-examination. Does this suggest a lack of conviction on the poet's part? It is possible that some poets write about subjects that they do not thoroughly understand and create characters they do not know and cannot believe in? The evidence certainly suggests that this is quite possible. A further observation along these lines concerns those poets who consistently fell back on their own personal histories for material. Usually, I was of the opinion that their lives did not warrant this excessive attention.

I hope that my response will contribute to your survey. I look forward to its results.

Ward Justin
High School English Teacher
Alhambra, California

Dear Reaper:

I was delighted to receive your challenging list of questions and the new anthologies several months ago. As you might guess, I liberally shared their contents with each of my five classes (155 students). After we got over the initial confusion as to what constituted a "young American poet," many lively discussions about the introductions and the poems ensued. But why the initial confusion? Let me give you an example to illustrate what I mean. A fifteen year-old student raised his hand and said "Herbert Scott's 54! That's young?" Another student added, "That's older than my father! And I don't think he was *ever* young!" Well, you see my point. So let me go on to share some of our other discoveries.

The introductions, which should have been helpful (and especially so for younger readers), were not. I copied all three of these prose documents, passed them out in my classes, and asked my students to write a brief analysis of each. Responses ranged from single sentences to substantial paragraphs to one page that was left blank but for a large, ominous question mark at its center. Some of the more memorable responses included one student's reaction to the logic, or lack of it (we had just studied logic in exposition earlier in the term), in the Wampeter introduction. This student wrote "I have not read anything by Mr. Auden, but the writer here seems to make him say something he *didn't* say. That's not right!" Another wrote that Smith and Bottoms (in Morrow) were being overly apologetic when they referred to their editing as "a tissue of compromises." The student went on to say "I'm afraid I wouldn't want these guys working for *me* as salesmen." And one student from fourth period was deeply offended by Anthony Hecht's assessment of The Average Reader.

As you know, in referring to Randall Jarrell, Hecht asserts that "most readers would rather encounter poetry in an anthology than in its pure form in a single volume by a single author. Both timidity and a certain prudential canniness tell them that a selection of any size is a hedge against being completely wrong, will save them from being a complete fool who has wasted every cent of his or her investment." This student was puzzled by Hecht's use of the word "pure," and her puzzlement was almost unanimously shared by the members of her class and other classes I queried. There was general agreement, too, that "a certain prudential canniness" was an example of gobbledygook. Finally, most agreed that Mr. Hecht was simply mistaken. As one student who might be speaking for an overwhelming majority put it: "I would much rather spend more time with one or two good small books than spend five minutes each on all of these poets! After awhile, they all sound the same to me."

As for the students' reaction to the poems themselves, let me offer a brief overview.

The students were eager to follow any poem that suggested or portrayed sex, though they disapproved of the suggestion of incest. They preferred action in poems and were frequently disappointed. They found little humor in either anthology (with notable exception in Wampeter of Russell Edson), and this, too, was disappointing. They quickly tired of Family poems—what so-and-so did, and how so-and-so's mother felt about it, etc.—and poems that seemed to, as one student put it, "go nowhere." They almost unanimously enjoyed Rita Dove's "Parsley" (in Wampeter) because it told a good story and seemed "current." More than a few students modestly thought they could at least equal the performances of many poets represented in the anthologies.

Finally, they wondered why the Morrow anthology had photographs of the poets while the Wampeter anthology did not. I suggested that the Morrow people probably had more money than the Wampeter people for such things, and this seemed to satisfy them. Then a student in fifth period wondered why so many of the poets looked so unhappy. "Sullen" was a popular description. One student said "if *my* picture and poems were being published in a book, I'd be pretty happy!" I didn't know what to say to this. Some of the boys did insist that Carolyn Forché was "a fox," and many students loved Diane Ackerman's photo in front of an airplane. A number expressed a desire to fly her.

Austin Auberge
KGBO
Detroit, Michigan

Dear Reaper:

Ok! So I'm late! But hey, baby, these Po-EnPsyche's have been tested *under fire!* How so? First, I read them, *every* page. I made copious notes. I chose my favorites, read excerpts over the air, and invited my listeners to call in. They did. And according to those callers, which poets excavated the Poetry Happy Hole? Ai, for one. And a hands-down favorite, really. Her lines, her stories, have muscle and wounded hearts. Carolyn Forché's a winner, too. She's so *timely*, so *aware!* Denis Johnson was popular, as were Heather McHugh, Sharon Olds, and Gary Soto. And Jim Tate and Russell Edson are always good for high voltage. Don Johnson got a lot of praise, most of it from lady callers who referred to his poems as the work of one buff dude. Toward the end of my survey, one caller expressed delight and surprise that the star of *Miami Vice* wrote poetry!! Well, radio surveys aren't perfect, Reap!

On the down side, well . . . that's just about everybody else. Especially alien were the poems of Alfred Corn (he's just too deep for humans) and Tom Lux (whose last name sure reflects his poetic good fortune in getting into so many of these shopping cart collections).

Ok. So much for the rating game. The fact is most of the poems don't say well. They're so *expository*. Know what I mean? I've been hosting this poetry show for five years now, and it's tough to find poems—and poets—that *say* well. One caller called it The Poetry of Implosion. Maybe he's got something.

Of course, hosting this show has made me a history buff of sorts. You know, literary trends and such-like. As you know and I know (and those who shell out the big bucks for these bombs will soon know), history tells us that most of the poems—95%—are no good. No sense in anybody getting nasty about it. It's just so. But, hell! It keeps people working, right? I couldn't help but notice that if you combine these two books, they read (most of the time) like an Interlocking Directory. You know what I mean, right? Listen, they publish each other in their magazines and invite each other to writing conferences; they meet up at symposiums and conferences where they eat together, drink together, sleep together, and praise one another's rise up the Po-corporate Ladder. Sure, the Po-corporation is a lot smaller than Chrysler or Citibank or Merrill Lynch, but the same corporate ethics of the Closed Club apply.

Which is all by way of saying that there are few surprises—and many blind spots —in these anthologies. I hasten to add that not all corporate ethics are bad. They start to get hairy when we take them too seriously.

Listen! It's been buff sharing these tomes on my tune-line. I'm on the air in ten minutes, so I'm signing off the printed page. Look forward to the next issue and other responses.

Scythe on, Reaper!

Nora Bodie
Chairman, The Reading Club
Columbus, Ohio

Dear Reaper,

Our club has studied the questions you sent and the two volumes for review, *New American Poets of the 80's* published by Wampeter Press and *The Morrow Anthology of Younger American Poets*, and decided that the only way to make sense of nearly 900 poems, including those printed in both anthologies, was some sort of classification. As readers of *The Reaper*, we detected the fuzziness of Anthony Hecht's comments on lyric poetry in his introduction to the Morrow anthology and yet would agree that most of the poems represented in both anthologies are lyric, whether spoken or sung. Because so many seem to be rather flatly spoken by their authors, it is hard to distinguish among them. So, taking a page from *The Reaper's* program, we have looked for narratives.

We have found that about 10 per cent of the poems in the Morrow and about 12 per cent in the Wampeter are more or less narrative; only about half of these do we like. You might agree that the percentages themselves are impressive; we expected them to be lower. The anthologists, who have been gracious enough to include themselves, seem to go for a strong narrative line in their own poems. We wondered why this preference was not also an aesthetic criterion in selecting even more poems that were narrative in structure. We are sure the anthologists were just trying to be objective.

Having decided to focus on some 25 poems in the Morrow anthology and 20 in the Wampeter, we began to see if distinctions could be made among them and learned that they really could—not only clear ones which shed some light on contemporary poetry and even on the reason poets may have lost their readers (except for readers like us who, by the way, prefer to discuss individual volumes rather than bulky anthologies).

We discovered four categories among the narrative poems, two of which are rather closely linked. These two are poems that narrate an incident, one subjectively and the other objectively. Category three includes poems in the voice of an imaginary speaker. And category four is the balladlike poem. Most of the poems fit into categories one and two, the majority in number one.

In the poem that narrates an incident subjectively, something has happened to the poet, represented quite clearly by the "I" of the poem, which he or she must tell us as a story or illustrative anecdote. This seems close to the lyric as Wordsworth wrote it. Outstanding examples from the Morrow anthology are "Under the Boathouse" by David Bottoms, "Black Silk" by Tess Gallagher (also in the Wampeter anthology), "Salmon" by Jorie Graham, "Cruelty" by Terry Hummer, "Old Dog, New Dog" by Sydney Lea, "Winter Stars" by Larry Levis (in the Wampeter, too), "My Happiness" by Greg Pape, "Mrs. Applebaum's Sunday Dance Class" by Phillip Schultz, "The Knife" by Richard Tillinghast, and "Burning Shit at An Khe" by Bruce Weigl. In the Wampeter anthology there are "Travelling Light" by Alice Fulton, "The Hug" by Tess Gallagher, "After Labor Day" by Sydney Lea, "Conception" by Sandra McPherson, "A Story" by Susan Mitchell, "Behind Grandma's House" by Gary Soto, "Sunday Graveyard" by Maura Stanton, and "This Tree" by William Hathaway. In these poems the incident is narrated from the poet's point of view to reflect a new understanding of him or herself. Like Wordsworth, he or she is speaking not only to humanity but for humanity; the poet's personal experience has been understood as universal. It could even be that narration itself is incidental; it may simply be an alternative to exposition or argument.

The objectively told incident is, perhaps, a fishy category, yet among the narrative poems there were some, a handful in both volumes, that appeared, at least, to attempt to tell a story in fictional and not lyric terms. This is important, we think, a serious distinction. What tells us it really exists are two poems which may be both subjective and objective: Lynn Emanuel's "Flying Trout While Drunk" in the Morrow and David Wojahn's "Satin Doll" in the Wampeter. The poet is present, especially in Wojahn's poem, and is acknowledged as in control, but the focus is on someone else's life, a character almost, although in Emanuel's poem it is her mother and in Wojahn's his aunt. The overwhelming emotion of each poem, however, comes from an understanding of somebody other than the poet. The following examples don't appear to include the poet at all.

In the Morrow they are "Yellow Light" by Garrett Hongo, "Answering Dance" by William Pitt Root, "The Enormous Aquarium" by Sherod Santos (also in the Wampeter), and "The Green Horse" by Bin Ramke. In the Wampeter we find "Providence" by David St. John, "Spit" by C. K. Williams, and "Black Dog, Red Dog" by Stephen Dobyns.

We were really very interested in the number of poems written in the voices of imaginary speakers, since all of us know Browning's dramatic lyrics and monologues and his cast of historical characters who sing and speechify. We were pleased to see the form still exists and yet happy, too, that it hasn't gone crazy; at least, the editors haven't overloaded on it. And we realized that, as with Frost's and Browning's and Robinson's people, if a character is going to speak, a story of some sort is going to be told. In the Morrow these poems stand out: "She Didn't Even Wave" by Ai, "The Armorer's Daughter" by Debora Greger, "The Ghost of a Ghost" by Brad Leithauser, "Weldon Kees in Mexico, 1965" by David Wojahn, and "In the Turkish Ward" by Peter Balakian. In the Wampeter there are "Einstein's Exile in an Old Dutch Winter" by Norman Dubie, "Shadow Shadow" by Roger Weingarten, and "Josie Bliss, October, 1971" by Carolyne Wright. We wondered about "Cavafy in Redondo" by Mark Jarman but we couldn't understand where Cavafy was— Redondo?—and what he was doing there.

Finally, the most interesting and rarest were those poems in both anthologies that really linked up with an older form of narrative poetry, not the highly civilized epic but the ballad, the folk poem. Like the old ballads, these poems seemed to bring news of the world, of parts unknown and yet familiar, in a highly concentrated form. We can't say that any is the equal of "Sir Patrick Spens" or "Lord Randall" but again we think their presence among the narrative poems suggests a separate category which we have decided to call the balladlike poem. In the Morrow they are "Introduction of the Shopping Cart" by Gerald Costanzo, "Mountain Bride" by Robert Morgan, "The Morning They Shot Tony Lopez" by Gary Soto, and

"A Funny Joke" by Leon Stokesbury. In the Wampeter they are "Parsley" by Rita Dove, "The Moment for Which There is No Name" by Morton Marcus, "Put Your Mother on the Ceiling" by Greg Pape, and "Fossils, Metals, and the Blue Limit" by Richard Tillinghast. Actually, the last is as much epic as ballad and deserves to be in a category by itself.

We hope you will find this an adequate response to both anthologies. As for the other paraphernalia and apparatus of the books —the pictures, the so-called criteria, the bios—they didn't interest us much. We liked these few poems and could understand their purpose. If more contemporary poetry was written like them, then maybe more people would read it.

The Death of the Lyric
The Achievement of Louis Simpson

Because no one else seems able to state the obvious about our current situation in poetry, *The Reaper* is willing to restore order where debilitating chaos reigns. It is time, really, it is *past* time, to admit that the lyric poem is dead. We can no longer afford to speak of it—that poem of predetermined emotion, that contemporary *so what* poem—as we would speak of a coveted jewelled music box. The tune of this form-in-isolation is clogged with sand.

What does *The Reaper* mean by "form-in-isolation?" He means that the lyric mode, as it is practiced today, has little to do with the tradition of lyric poetry and even less to do with modern life. He targets here the dominant poem of our time, the defective off-spring, whether in traditional meter or not, of confessionalism, deep imagism, and the essay-as-poem.

By now, all of you know this tame rat well. In the typical lyric poem, the first person pronoun dominates. In the opening lines it vies with conventional description for the reader's attention. The central complaint appears, achieving a pitch like a whine. Now and then, there's an anecdote to stimulate the reader's lagging interest (the more daring formula lyrics begin with anecdote), but the "I" desperately veers from the challenge of story to relapse into a studied recitation of prefigured emotion. Sometimes the third person pronoun is employed for the sake of objectivity, but since character is never fleshed out, he / she sounds like the "I." Sometime "we" is used to suggest communal authority, but the same problem that thwarts the use of the third person impedes the success of "we."

This sorry condition reminds *The Reaper* of the prize cow that amiably grazed too close to the edge of a cliff. Taking a step to procure one more tasty morsel, she plummeted into a crevasse and broke her neck, ending up wedged, upside down, between the rocky walls. The coyotes couldn't reach her; the vultures did a bad job. A week passed, and by then the carcass was overripe. The neighbors raised hell, and the cow's owner had devil of a time chemically speeding up the decomposition. Today's lyric poem is a lot like that cow.

Traditionally the lyric conveyed the subjective interpretation of human feeling, a mood, or idea. Today it contains emotion devoid of content, as if an expression of sincerity alone could sustain any poem, and may take the shape of meditative monologues, sentimental descriptive verses, and wooden rehashings of philosophical conceits, conceived by far better minds and turned inside out and betrayed by the solipsism that is the contemporary lyric's trademark. It encourages its practitioners to think small and settle for less.

A look through the pages of most contemporary literary magazines provides damning evidence that this is so. These lyrics argue that sincerity need not communicate a vision to the reader, one that the reader can enter and share. They argue that one can share a vision in the same way that one shares gossip. They also house dead language, poor sentences chopped into poor lines and called intricate rhythms. Which they are not. They do not remotely sound like the words that real people in real situations would ever say. Most readers understood this years ago and turned to prose for the stories, the insights into their lives, which have largely vanished from poetry. These readers have consistently rejected the dominant poem of our time—the lyric.

Contemporary practitioners continue to struggle, zippered snugly into their sentimental lyric suits. However, there are heartening indications that a restlessness, previously isolated in scattered pockets, is gaining wider circulation in our poetry. This restlessness, akin to a snake shedding its skin, is always present in the work of superior poets, and even in the dark age of the rotting lyric, one can point to a few exemplary careers that have developed in opposition to the general malaise. Louis Simpson's career provides such an example.

Simpson's first three books, *The Arrivistes: Poems 1940-1949*, *Good News of Death and Other Poems*, and *A Dream of Governors*, amply proclaimed their author's formal expertise in the lyric. But given the poetry of the period, they also cleaved uncharacteristically to subjects. At their best, especially in the poems about World War II, their language struggles to break through their elegant façades. Their energy resists the simple goal to sing beautifully and tends toward a narrative, in ballads like "Carentan O Carentan" and "Memories of a Lost War," where the song is in service to the story.

The process constitutes a long and fruitful struggle throughout the body of Simpson's early work, and the tension between forms has given us some of the most important poems of our time.

In *A Dream of Governors*, published in 1959, Simpson tries his first extended narrative poem—"The Runner." It is a highly dramatic and successful elaboration of what appears to be, because of a prefatory note, a story from Simpson's World War II experience. It is in iambic pentameter and adheres to most conventions of narrative in that form, in dialogue, description, and characterization. Referring to it in a recent interview, Simpson claims that now he would cast it in his identifiable free verse style, the rhythmically flatter but tonally subtler three and four beat line. *The Reaper* thinks this is an incorrect view of "The Runner." It is, however, a correct view of Simpson himself and his way of writing. Simpson knows what sounds like Simpson.

In his fourth volume, *At the End of the Open Road* (1963), which received the Pulitzer Prize, Simpson broke through to a narrative expression that is closer to his current one in the overlooked poem, "The Marriage of Pacahontas." This eleven page poem in eight sections begins with introductory stanzas telling us that the episodes to follow are taken from Captain John Smith's *Generall Historie of Virginia, New England, and the Summer Isles.* The introduction does more, too. By focusing on an unusual aspect of Smith's character, his "theatrical / Extravagant spirit," Simpson succeeds in overcoming our prejudice toward the Great White Settler Among the Savages presented in stale accounts in grade school. Listen to the following extrapolated from a Smith letter to a duchess.

> "When I was slave to the Turkes,
> The beauteous Lady Tragabigzanda
> Did all she could to secure me.
> When I overcame the Bashaw of Nalbrits,
> The charitable Lady Callamata
> Supplyed my necessities.
> In the utmost of many necessities,
> That blessed Pocahontas,
> The great King's daughter of Virginia,
> Oft saved my life."

Suddenly the historical figure of one dimension is a vain man attempting to shine in the eyes of a perceived better. From this witty beginning we proceed into section one where Smith, in captivity, is presented to King Powhatan by his people. The community stages a harrowing feast in Smith's honor after which two stones are rolled out for the purpose of laying his head thereon and beating his brains out.

> Pocahontas, the King's dearest daughter,
> When no entreaty could prevail,
> Got his head in her arms,
> And laid her own upon his to save him from death.
> Whereat the Emperor was contented

He should live to make him hatchets,
And her, bells, beads, and copper.

Thus section one ends with a resolution for an uneasy cohabitation.
Sections two through five chronicle the tension and erosion of that
truce.

In section two Smith is confronted by thirty young women run-
ning naked out of the woods "crowding, pressing, and hanging
about him, / Crying, 'Love you not me?'" A European, not born to
these woods, the experience torments him. In section three, subti-
tled "A Dialogue of Peace and War," Powhatan attempts to convince
Smith to leave his weapons aboard ship: "What will it avail you to
take by force / What you may quickly have by love?" Smith agrees to
Powhatan's plea in spite of the fact that many of Powhatan's people
have already violated the truce. But in the fourth section Pocahon-
tas, a migratory victim caught between two cultures, again rescues
the colonists by warning Smith of a plot to kill them. In section five
she is rewarded by suffering incarceration at the hands of Captain
Argall, who would use her to pay a debt and forge his own peace
with her father. Smith intervenes and rescues her, and in section six
she is married to John Rolfe. The assimilation of the native is com-
plete. In section seven, we see the ramifications of this. The once
formidable Powhatan shares a pipe, laughter, and small talk with the
English king.

In the closing section, a first person narrator dreams of the
woods of Virginia, of what was and what is lost.

Give up your naked ways,
Except a few green leaves,
your cunning ambush where the coney plays.

Put on a skirt and hood.
Marry perhaps an English gentleman.
Though never English, you may still be good.

When I set out on my journey

It was high summer,
But now it was cold and snow lay on the ground.

I came to the great hall
Where Powhatan was sitting, with his braves
Beneath him in two rows along the wall.

I spoke. They seemed to hear.
They did not speak or move.
Then suddenly they shouted.

And a wind
Rushed through the hall, the torches guttered out,
And the night was filled with sound.

In this extraordinary poem the lyric is everywhere and accessible, serving an episodic narrative in which the poet, and narrator, are appropriately invisible. In order to accomplish this, a poet must be able to see his own life in the context of the lives of others; he must also be able to isolate, highlight, and string together the essential fragments of his characters' experience. This is why Simpson is able to convey the sense, in two hundred and seventy-eight lines, that we have learned all that there is to know about these characters. It has taken good prose writers much longer to tell as much, and *The Reaper* contends that none have quite come up to this account.

Two years after the appearance of *At the End of the Open Road*, in a short essay that originally appeared in *Harper's* Simpson clearly acknowledged his own need to move beyond the confinement of the lyric by expressing dissatisfaction with where poetry had taken us so far. "Most poetry," he wrote, "is mere fantasy; most prose is merely reporting the surface of things. We are still waiting for the poetry of feeling, words as common as a loaf of bread, which yet give off vibrations."

In the section of new poems in his 1965 *Selected Poems*, the poem "Stumpfoot on 42nd Street" shows Simpson's dissatisfaction with the poetry he described in *Harper's* and the possible solution to the problem. For Simpson, this poem might be more accurately called his deepening understanding of Wordsworth's "reek of the human."

Stumpfoot on 42nd Street

A Negro sprouts from the pavement like an asparagus.
One hand beats a drum and cymbal;
He plays a trumpet with the other.

He flies the American flag;
When he goes walking, from stump to stump,
It twitches, and swoops, and flaps.

Also, he has a tin cup which he rattles;
He shoves it right in your face.
These freaks are alive in earnest.

He is not embarrassed.
It is for you to feel embarrassed,
Or God, or the way things are.

Therefore he plays the trumpet
And therefore he beats the drum.

2

I can see myself in Venezuela,
With flowers, and clouds in the distance.
The mind tends to drift.

But Stumpfoot stands near a window
Advertising cameras, trusses, household utensils.
The billboards twinkle. The time
Is 12:26.

O why don't angels speak in the infinite
To each other? Why this confusion,
These particular bodies—

Eros with clenched fists, sobbing and cursing?

The time is 12:26.
The streets lead on in burning lines
And giants tremble in electric chains.

3

I can see myself in the middle of Venezuela
Stepping in a nest of ants.
I can see myself being eaten by ants.

My ribs are caught in a thorn bush
And thought has no reality.
But he has furnished his room

With a chair and table.
A chair is like a dog, it waits for man.
He unstraps his apparatus,

And now he is taking off his boots.
He is easing his stumps,
And now he lighting a cigar.

It seems that a man exists
Only to say, Here I am in person.

Mere poetic fantasy here, in which "the mind tends to drift," is interrupted by the reality of "Stumpfoot." Modern dilemmas like the dissociation of sensibility are here, along with the alienation of the self. Eros is confused and the imagination would place the poet in a distant clime to be devoured, like the missionary in Eliot's *The Cocktail Party*, by ants, merely to feel something genuine. But Stumpfoot keeps returning to the poem, requiring more than the portrayal in part one. The thought of that alienated sensibility has no reality set beside Stumpfoot, whose chair is more real, apparatus, boots, and cigar are more real than anything else evoked in the poem, besides the time, 12;26, and the places, 42nd Street and Stumpfoot's room. As understated as they are, the final two lines are as authoritative as Whitman's "Who touches this touches a man."

The Simpson of this poem is recognizable as the Simpson who is writing today. He has two muses. Whitman is the muse of his lyric poetry, and is most problematical for him, first, because Simpson has understood that Whitman's vision was not of a nation but of single man—himself; and second, because the vision of Whitman's America, as we tend to perceive it, has failed. Whitman's open road, as Simpson points out, "goes to the used-car lot." But Simpson also writes, "At the end of the open road we come to ourselves." Who are we, then? There is a deeply disillusioned side to Simpson's view of America, especially when he looks at California or at his current residence, Long Island, and of Europe, too, as it comes to resemble America. How Simpson has responded to the failure of the lyric vision has been his increasing involvement in narrative poetry, but with many returns to the lyric, as if, having conveyed human feeling through fictional characters and settings and actions, he were able at times to return to the lyric's subjective elasticity.

The muse of Simpson's narrative poetry is Chekhov, who leads Simpson to the imagined Russia of his ancestors, with its very real Cossacks and Nazis, and to his own Jewishness, something he has admitted not to have really contacted until the age of 17 when he left his childhood home of Jamaica for New York City where he met his mother's relatives. This Russia first appears in a couple of poems in *At the End of the Open Road*, "A Story About Chicken Soup" and "The Troika." For readers of Simpson, it is not news that finding this subject was a breakthrough for him. But even in his latest book, *The Best Hour of the Night*, where there is only the poem "Akhmatova's Husband" to recall this breakthrough, Chekhov remains the muse. The lyric voice of Whitman has been altogether muted—killed, perhaps, or perhaps transformed.

It is in his 1971 book *Adventures of the Letter I* that Simpson begins to show most fully how much he has come to distrust the lyric and trust the narrative. Also, the Russia of Louis Simpson stands out most clearly, and so do Chekhov's warmth and sense of tragedy in Simpson's characterizations.

It would be presumptuous for *The Reaper* to apply his own check-list from issue number 11 on how to write a narrative poem to one of Simpson's best poems from this book, but *The Reaper* is nothing if not presumptuous. At a time when there is talk about every poem's essential narrativity, because a poem is linear, because one thing follows another, and syntax unfolds like a story, it is necessary to show what a real narrative poem looks like or can look like, today.

A Son of the Romanovs

> This is Avram the cello-mender,
> the only Jewish sergeant
> in the army of the Tsar.
> One day he was mending cellos
> when they shouted, "The Tsar is coming,
> everyone out for inspection!"
> When the Tsar saw Avram marching
> with Russians who were seven feet tall,
> he said, "He must be a genius.
> I want that fellow at headquarters."
>
> Luck is given by god.
> A wife you must find for yourself.
> So Avram married a rich widow
> who lived in a house in Odessa.
> The place was filled with music . . .
> Yasnaya Polyana with noodles.
>
> One night in the middle of a concert
> they hear a knock at the door.
> So Avram went. It was a beggar,
> a Russian, who had been blessed

by God—that is, he was crazy.
And he said, "I am a natural son
of the Grand Duke Nicholas."

And Avram said, "Eat.
I owe your people a favor."
And he said, "My wife is complaining
we need someone to open the door."
So Nicholas stayed with them for years.
Who ever heard of Jewish people
with a footman?

And then the Germans came. Imagine
the scene—the old people
holding on to their baggage,
and the children—they've been told it's a game,
but they don't believe it.
Then the German says, "Who's this?"
pointing at Nicholas,
"he doesn't look like a Jew."
And he said, "I'm the natural son
of the Grand Duke Nicholas."
And they saw he was feeble-minded,
and took him away too, to the death-chamber.

"He could have kept his mouth shut,"
said my Grandmother,
"but what can you expect.
All of those Romanovs were a little bit crazy."

First, there is the double sense of *beginning, middle, and end* to this
story. There is the tale the poem tells in its form of family folklore,
beginning with the relative Avram, the arrival of the simpleton
Nicholas, and Grandmother's final comment, which implies that the
tale is hers. Also, and just as important, there is the larger story of

history, which includes Jewish life under the Tsars, in this case the last Tsar, the holocaust that ended an entire way of life in Europe for the Jews, and then, as often happens in Simpson's poems, the denouement in the new world. Because of these two integrated modes, the poem seems twice as whole.

Observation in the poem is cunning, because detail apparently is given in a haphazard way, with only the intention of moving the story along, as an older relative might tell an important family anecdote. But that is partly because of the subtle weave of Simpson's narrative. The Russians are "seven feet tall" obviously in comparison to Avram; music and food are mixed together; and there is a continual commentary that hints at the character of the narrator ("Luck is given by God. / A wife you must find for yourself." and "blessed / by God—that is, he was crazy.") that points to the Grandmother as the storyteller, allowing the poet to be witness through her eyes and her listener, too.

As for *compression of time*, the lives of Avram and Nicholas and the Jews of Russia and their survivors in America are given in 46 lines. Part of this is because we know the history, that it can be done; but Nicholas' and Avram's stories as they intersect with history could have taken much longer in prose. Though Simpson's verse has been accused of flatness, it is working basically with a four and three beat line. Incidentally, this is the rhythm he perfected in his earlier ballads and is still his strongest meter.

Characters are important in this story and their gestures develop them and produce other logical gestures. It is logical for Avram to invite this son of the Duke into his house, even though his gratitude might be mixed with pity and another intention. Logical that because he is married to a rich widow he would want to indulge her desire for "a footman." But the most horribly logical *containment* of character here is the rationale of the Germans who, hearing Nicholas identify himself as he always has, take him, too, "to the death-chamber." Even Grandmother's comment both contains and is contained by her character. The Romanovs symbolize all gentiles, and their madness with regard to Jews is understated when considering one harmless member of their race.

This sense of *containment* is, of course, created by the *illumination of private gestures*; here, it is what people say to one another. Avram defers to his wife in the presence of a simpleton, "My wife is complaining / we need someone to open the door." The Tsar witlessly impressed by Avram's size among his taller soldiers announces, "He must be a genius. / I want that fellow at headquarters." And, finally, Grandmother's remark is wrenching in its pathos—"He could have kept his mouth shut."

Understatement is the eloquent shrug one hears in Simpson's tone, "And then the Germans came." The first time we hear it is in "A Story About Chicken Soup" in which he states about people like the cello-mender, ". . . the Germans killed them. / I know it's in bad taste to say it, / But it's true. The Germans killed them all." This is not merely an American gesture of know-nothingism. It is this very sense of understatement that successfully links the private and public, the personal and historical dramas in Simpson's poetry.

It is also this view of the private world's place in the larger tragic scene that produces and benefits from Simpson's *humor*. The Reaper has described humor as "an exploitation of intimacy." Here it comes when the beggar appears at the door, announcing that he is "a natural son / of the Grand Duke Nicholas"; thus, he will escape one small holocaust only to meet his fate in the larger one. Thus, too, the narrator can comment wryly, "Who ever heard of Jewish people / with a footman?" Grandmother can make her comment about the Romanovs, too, unconsciously implying much that the maker of this poem would have us infer consciously.

The poem's *location* is the Russia of Simpson's family stories. Specifically, it is Odessa, the South Ukrainian port on the Black Sea, which suggests prosperity, a healthful climate, an enviable place far from the miserable winters of Moscow and Leningrad. The location has become even more Simpson's than his current situation on Long Island.

The Reaper calls for *memorable characters* in a narrative poem, and it its clear that Avram the cello-mender and Nicholas the footman are memorable. So is Grandmother, with her brief, final, but important appearance. We can point to many others, too, in Simpson's poetry from this book to the present. Not since E. A. Robinson has an American poet populated his poems so richly.

The *compelling subject* in this poem is the fate of Russian Jews, and within the context of Simpson's work, their fate contrasts with the life of their survivors and others living in the new world, the dull suburbs of Simpson's other narrative poems—Long Island, with its petty prejudices, its monotonous appetites, its lack of vitality. This other world is poised by Simpson against the Russian one and presents the most problematic aspect of Simpson's poetry—why the lyric strain that can even be heard in some of the Russian pieces, like "Dvonya," has vanished altogether.

Russia or an imagined Russia is not the only source of Simpson's poetry. There is also his childhood in Jamaica. In the preface to *Searching for the Ox* (1976) Simpson tells of a recurring dream in which he stands on a Kingston beach of white sand. The sand is fine and there are "shells of all shapes and colors." Simpson stoops to pick up these shells as fast as he can for he "shall soon have to leave." This image of a child desperately striving to gather some imperishable totems of the known world before the onslaught of a malevolent, evicting force is at the heart of this poet's life work. In the preface he goes on to discuss his childhood in Jamaica. "Isolation turned me to reading stories and poems. It was stories I was after in either case; I didn't want fine emotions as much as I wanted something to happen to break the silence of the island." This is the restlessness of the storyteller, the keeper of a culture's history and soul, the narrative poet.

The book itself, laid out in four parts, constitutes a long journey on which the narrator comes, at last, to recognize the virtues of that first place, where he yearned for something to happen. The four poems of section one, "Venus in the Tropics," "Dinner at the Sea-

View Inn," "The Psyche of Riverside Drive," and "Lorenzo" display some of the most condensed, and some of the best, talk you will find in contemporary poetry. The author's young stand-in, Peter, reappears from earlier poems to piece together the stories of those important to him by virtue of what they do and say. In "Venus in the Tropics" he listens to the voices of his stepmother and grand-mother and ends up poolside reading and dreaming of sex. In "Dinner at the Sea-View Inn" he botches a date with his girlfriend and her parents and concludes the evening back in his apartment "Lying in bed, hands clasped beneath his head, / listening. . ." Finally, in "The Psyche of Riverside Drive," the listener comes to some conclusions, the necessary prelude to directed action. He vis-its an old professor who tells him "that the visible world was a dream." This doesn't charm the former student much, and he con-cludes that "the Professor was a dream. / How could I, he wondered, ever have listened to this?" Earlier, walking down the corridor of the professor's building, he imagines the apartments to be cabins on a ship—an image of passage—"But all the voyage would be inward." This recapitulates the conclusion of At the End of the Open Road, but it adds something, too. It includes the mature and demanding con-viction that the voyage inward will be facilitated not by striking im-ages or by song alone, but by coming to a full awareness of the players in one's life drama. To accomplish this, one must listen and observe; one cannot expect to fit the players to a preconceived point of view. In "Lorenzo" the young aspiring writer lives abroad for a time, but rather than giving us the sensitive perceptions of himself in a foreign landscape, he provides a haunting portrait of a writer who knew D. H. Lawrence and, in a miraculous transformation at the end of the poem, of Lawrence himself.

The book's second section finds the narrator, now in full com-mand of a heightened sensibility, back in New York where drama never sleeps. He escapes "making the millstone go round and round" by walking out after five years in the publishing business. With good humor he comments on visiting a wealthy friend who has one room decorated solely by a tropical aquarium. The narrator

notices one fish adhering to the side of the tank, and the host tells
him that its job is sanitation.

> When I thought of my one and a half rooms
> with the Salvation Army furniture,
> I could have applied for the job myself.
>
> "The Stevenson Poster"

A poet-historian, he moves through the city recording memorable
encounters with, among others, an anxious woman, who is con-
vinced that people are saying things about her, with a rejected au-
thor who confides that a famous novelist has been stealing his ideas
for years, with an old alley-dweller who claims that he served in the
Seventh Cavalry, with middleaged Tim Flanagan who lives with his
recently widowed sister, and with Mandelbaum who works at the
Hospital for Joint Diseases. It is in conversation with the last that
the issue of the romantic versus the realistic is addressed; this issue,
along with lyric versus the narrative, runs through Simpson's work.
In this poem we can also see how successfully Simpson has come to
make human speech resonate.

OK For Keats

> "Keats said that truth is beauty—
> I say just the opposite.
> When I see truth in front of me
> it has a terrible appearance."

> Thus spake Mandelbaum,
> sitting on the beach.
> He was thin and somewhat sallow
> from his work at the Hospital for Joint Diseases—
> the hairs on his body glistening
> like fish scales, flat and wet.

> "Beauty was OK for Keats,
> but ever since Buchenwald and Auschwitz

people have pictures in the back of their head—
emaciated human beings,
bodies stacked up like wood,
photographs of rooms full of shoes
and clothing arranged in piles.
Not to mention the atom bomb,
faces and bodies exposed to radiation.
That is truth. Where is the beauty?

I couldn't waste my time
reading English. When I raised an objection
they would tell me it was art
so it didn't have to make sense.

It's been a long time,"
he said, "but I seem to recall—
didn't Keats have medical training?
Didn't he work in a hospital?"

"He was a surgeon's apprentice."

"There you are. He ought to have known better."

Do we smile at this because Mandelbaum is a caricature and a
fool, made physically unbeautiful himself with his fishscale hairs
and exposed body at the beach? But the assertion of Keats's ode is
questionable and has been especially for the modern period. Auden
himself stated that there is a discrepancy between the beauty of the
Greeks on their hilltop and the truth of the barbarians at the base.
Has Mandelbaum trivialized the two great horrors of our age by
quickly listing evidence of one, then adding the other with "Not to
mention the atom bomb," i.e. not to mention the unmentionable?
Yes, in part—but that is the character of Mandelbaum. The quiet
confirmation of the statement in the poem's second to last line, that
Keats did have medical training, suggests that Mandelbaum, though
a lost cause with respect to literature, has been heard by the other
person, most likely the poet himself.

In the final two sections of this collection the narrator moves out into the suburbs succinctly recording the characters, with their own unique ambitions and grievances, he moves among. The long title poem, oddly located in section three, is a summary of the narrator's scrupulous witnessing. It is also a profound lament for the world in which feeling is blunted by the onslaught of technology and an indictment of The Improvers who harness and direct it with arrogant insensitivity. Because narrative, the method of choice in these poems, provides the opportunities for such thorough study, the reader feels the camaraderie and the terror in his bones, and the indictment sticks. It is impossible to say this about the popular lyric poems of the time.

Caviare at the Funeral (1980) includes what have been so far Simpson's last major efforts on the subject of Russia, and an answer to those who might ask why he has chosen the subject. "Why Do You Write About Russia?" begins simply, "When I was a child / my mother told stories about the country / she came from." There are a number of excellent Russian poems here, but the poem *The Reaper* wants to discuss is a new world poem, one of Simpson's autobiographical memoir-poems that also point toward his narratives of suburban American life, those poems that have made him, for us, both our Robinson and Chekhov—in other words, an American original.

Sway

"Swing and sway with Sammy Kaye"

Everyone at Lake Kearney had a nickname:
there was a Bumstead, a Tonto, a Tex,
and, from the slogan of a popular orchestra,
two sisters, Swing and Sway.

Swing jitterbugged, hopping around
on the dance floor, working up a sweat.
Sway was beautiful. My heart went out to her
when she lifted her heavy rack of dishes
and passed through the swinging door.

She was engaged, to an enlisted man
who was stationed at Fort Dix.
He came once or twice on weekends
to see her. I tried talking to him,
but he didn't answer . . . out of stupidity
or dislike, I could not tell which.
In real life he was a furniture salesman.
This was the hero on whom she had chosen
to bestow her affections.

I told her of my ambition:
to write novels conveying the excitement
of life . . . the main building lit up
like a liner on Saturday night;
the sound of the band . . . clarinet,
saxophone, snare drum, piano.

He who would know your heart (America)
must seek it in your songs.

And the contents of your purse . . .
among Kleenex, aspirin,
chewing gum wrappers, combs, et cetera.
"Don't stop," she said, "I'm listening.
Here it is! flourishing her lighter.

≈

In the afternoon when the dishes were washed
and tables wiped, we rowed out on the lake.
I read aloud . . . *The Duino Elegies*,
while she reclined, one shapely knee up,
trailing a hand in the water.

She had chestnut-colored hair.
Her eyes were changing like the surface
with ripples and the shadows of clouds.

"Beauty," I read to her, "is nothing
but beginning of Terror we're still just able to bear."

≈

She came from Jersey, the industrial wasteland
behind which Manhattan suddenly rises.
I could visualize the street where she lived,
and see her muffled against the cold,
in galoshes, trudging to school.
Running about in tennis shoes
all through the summer . . .
I could hear the porch swing squeak
and see into the parlor.
It was divided by a curtain or screen . . .

"That's it," she said, "all but the screen.
There isn't any."

When she or her sister had a boyfriend
their mother used to stay in the parlor,
pretending to sew, and keeping an eye on them
like Fate.

At night she would lie awake
looking at the sky, spangled over.
Her thoughts were as deep and wide as the sky.
As time went by she had a feeling
of missing out . . . that everything
was happening somewhere else.

Some of the kids she grew up with
went crazy . . . like a car turning over and over.
One of her friends had been beaten
by the police. Some vital fluid
seemed to have gone out of him.
His arms and legs shook. Busted springs.

She said, "When you're a famous novelist
will you write about me?"

I promised . . . and tried to keep my promise.

Recently, looking for a toolbox,
I came upon some typewritten pages,
all about her. There she is
in a canoe . . . a gust of wind
rustling the leaves along the shore.
Playing tennis, running up and down the baseline.
Down by the boathouse, listening to the orchestra
playing "Sleepy Lagoon."

Then the trouble begins. I can never think of anything
to make the characters do.
We are still sitting in the moonlight
while she finishes her cigarette.
Two people go by, talking in low voices.
A car door slams. Driving off . . .
"I suppose we ought to go,"
I say.
          And she says, "Not yet."

The narrative structure here includes what Eric Auerbach calls a Homeric excursus. Between the moment Sway finds her lighter and the end of the poem, when she is not yet finished with her cigarette, the narration wanders, describing her and her relationship with the narrator. There is also the interpolation of her voice, commenting on his story and the excursus itself. It is like the voice that answers Mandelbaum in "OK for Keats" in the way it confirms and modulates the story. It is also, arguably, like the presence of Stumpfoot in "Stumpfoot on 42nd Street" which brings reality to bear and keeps the poet honest. The richness of Sway's characterization, the wistfulness of this relationship, and the pathos of the moment when the poet finds the old manuscript while looking for his toolbox are all quite clear. What might not be so clear, although it should be, is the originality of Simpson's narrative style.

A complaint against narrative poetry, including much recent narrative poetry, is that it does not tell a story as well as prose fiction; that is, one might prefer to read a story by Raymond Carver than a narrative poem by Louis Simpson, simply to compare two writers who have been regarded as similar—in one case by Simpson himself in an interview in *The Character of the Poet*. In fact, there is no short story writer who can do what Simpson does. What he does can only be compared to the narrations of a film, for example, one of Woody Allen's autobiographical movies, in which action is illuminated by commentary and vice versa. Action occurs in a stream of meditation, as significant imagery. Furthermore, the compressed time of a film is analogous to that of a narrative poem; yet again, the poem's compression is greater. Simpson has dealt with his inability to make characters do anything, as he describes in "Sway," by taking a meditative rather than a dramatic approach; thus, focusing on the gestures and speech of characters so that they are framed as images and creating suspense through apparent digressions (Auerbach's Homeric excursus), Simpson makes his own kind of drama. Sway's answer, "'Not yet,'" is charged with this accomplishment.

On the back cover of Simpson's most recent book, *The Best Hour of the Night* (1983), is a blurb that reads, "'A genuine lyrical writer of strength and loveliness.'" This is a typically innocuous testimonial, except that the definition of "lyrical" is in doubt, at least as *The Reaper* views Simpson's best poetry. If Whitman is the muse of his lyric poetry, what form does that inspiration take in Simpson's latest work?

The Best Hour of the Night is a book of life on Long Island, of life in the American middle class. Nostalgia for Russia is absent in this book. The characters are not named Avram or Adam Yankev, but Ed and Bernie and Jim Bandy. Curiously, though Whitman's sense of himself and his country may no longer have meaning for Simpson, even as satire, a new feeling for this failure has come into his work. Perhaps the only description of it can be "lyrical."

How to Live on Long Island

Lilco, $75.17;
Mastercard, $157.89;
Sunmark Industries, $94.03. . .

Jim is paying his bills.
He writes out a check
and edges it into the envelope
provided by the company.
They always make them too small.

The print in the little box
in the top right corner informs him:
"The Post Office will not deliver
mail without proper postage."
They seem to know that the public
is composed of thieves and half-wits.

He seals the last envelope,
licks a stamp, sticks it on,
and with a feeling of virtue,
a necessary task accomplished,
takes the checks out to the mailbox.

It's a cool, clear night in Fall,
lights flickering through the leaves.
He thinks, all these families
with their situation comedies:
husbands writing checks,
wives studying fund-raising,
children locked in their rooms

listening to the music that appeals to them,
remind me of . . . fireflies
that shine for a night and die.

Of all these similar houses
what shall be left? Not even stones.
One could almost understand the pharaohs
with their pyramids and obelisks.
Every month when he pays his bills
Jim Bandy becomes a philosopher.
The rest of the time he's OK.

Jim has a hobby: fishing.
Last year he flew to Alaska.
Cold the salmon stream,
dark the Douglas firs,
and the pure stars are cold.

A bear came out of the forest.
Jim had two salmon . . . he threw one
but the bear kept coming.
He threw the other . . . it stopped.

The fish that are most memorable
he mounts, with a brass plate
giving the name and place and date:
Chinook Salmon, Red Salmon,
Brown Trout, Grouper,
Barracuda, Hammerhead Shark.

They do a lot of drinking in Alaska.
He saw thirty or forty lying drunk
in the street. And on the plane. . .

They cannot stand living in Alaska,
and he cannot stand Long Island
without flying to Alaska.

Although all of Simpson's narrative innovations are present in this poem, there is also a rhythm of repetition that is stronger than in his previous narrative poetry. This is how it feels to be an American 100 years after Whitman, in which American restlessness to be on the road is expressed through flight. The irony is that one must return. The irony is that at the end of the open road we do come to ourselves, as Simpson predicted. As he has brought his poetry closer to home, back from his excursions to Russia and Jamaica and the past, he has relocated the original source of poetry. It is in the poet, whose impulse is toward the lyric. What Simpson has done for this poet is make him human again, by emphasizing narrative and the lyric in service to it. Simpson recognizes this reunion and homecoming, not without his typical mordancy, in the last poem of this book.

The Unwritten Poem

You will never write the poem about Italy.
What Socrates said about love
is true of poetry—where is it?
Not in beautiful faces and distant scenery
but in the one who writes and loves.

In your life here, on this street
where the houses from the outside
are all alike, and so are the people.
Inside, the furniture is dreadful—
floc on the walls, and huge color television.

To love and write unrequited
is the poet's fate. Here you'll need
all your ardor and ingenuity.
This is the front and these are the heroes—
a life beginning with "Hi!" and ending with "So long!"

You must rise to the sound of the alarm
and march to catch the 6:20—

watch as they ascend the station platform
and, grasping briefcases, pass beyond your gaze
and hurl themselves into the flames.

Louis Simpson's poetry over the last twenty-five years has done more to develop an American narrative than the poetry of any other writer. He is, and always has been, *the* late-modern example that comes first to *The Reaper*'s mind.

Appendix
Front Covers and Contents Pages

THE REAPER

Issue 1

CONTENTS

1

The Reaper is the great deleter, the one who
determines when the story ends. . .

CONTENTS

Coming in Issue #3:
    The Reaper's non-negotiable demands. . .

1

Issue 2

Issue 3

The Reaper is the great deleter, the
one who determines when the story ends...

CONTENTS

2

The Reaper is the great deleter, the
one who determines when the story ends...

CONTENTS

Erratum: In issue number 3 of *The Reaper*, on page 18,
line 25 of Aaron Fischer's "Bellini's 'St. Paul on the
Road to Damascus'" should read, "Two turn away. All
eyes."

Coming in issue number 5!
—An essay on contemporary fiction by Thomas
Wilhelmus
—*The Reaper* interviews the best young poets
in America

DON'T BE CAUGHT DEAD WITHOUT READING IT!

Issue 4

THE REAPER

THE REAPER

Issue 5

The Reaper is the great deleter, the
one who determines when the story ends...

CONTENTS

Coming in issue number 6!

—"I Have Seen, I Know," an essay on genuine and artificial
narrative poets.
—Poems by Bruce Beasley, Jonathan Holden, Larry Moffi, Paul
Nelson, Alison Fuller, Liam Rector, and others

DON'T BE CAUGHT DEAD WITHOUT READING IT!

No. 6

ACTUALITES.   211.

46.

?
THE REAPER

The Reaper is the great deleter, the
one who determines when the story ends...

CONTENTS

Coming in issue number 7!
—An essay on fiction by Thomas Wilhelmus
—Poems by Vern Rutsala, Jared Carter, and others;
 reviews by Dennis Sampson

DON'T BE CAUGHT DEAD WITHOUT READING IT!

Issue 6

Issue 7

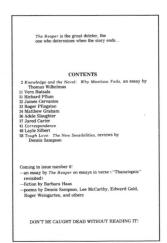

The Reaper is the great deleter, the
one who determines when the story ends...

CONTENTS

Coming in issue number 8!
—an essay by *The Reaper* on essays in verse ("Thanatopsis"
 revisited)
—fiction by Barbara Haas
—poems by Dennis Sampson, Lee McCarthy, Edward Gold,
 Roger Weingarten, and others

DON'T BE CAUGHT DEAD WITHOUT READING IT!

No. 7

THE REAPER

The Reaper is the great deleter, the
one who determines when the story ends...

CONTENTS

Coming in issue number 9!
—Dante in Dogtown
—poems by Jared Carter, George Hitchcock, Diane Reynolds,
Chris Semansky, Mark Anthony Mastro, R.T. Smith, Donald
Morrill, Pat Snee, Maurya Simon, Sheila Sanderson, and
others

DON'T BE CAUGHT DEAD WITHOUT READING IT!

Issue 8

No. 8

THE REAPER

Issue 9

No. 9

The Reaper

The Reaper is the great deleter, the
one who determines when the story ends...

CONTENTS

Coming in issue number 10!
—Donald Hall Assesses *The Reaper's* First 10 Issues
—an essay by Thomas Wilhelmus
—poems by Hayden Carruth, Jared Carter, Adele Slaughter,
Diane Reynolds, Donald Morrill, John Bakalis, and others...

DON'T BE CAUGHT DEAD WITHOUT READING IT!

The Reaper is the great deleter, the one who determines when the story ends . . .

CONTENTS

Issue 10

Issue 11

The Reaper is the great deleter, the one who determines when the story ends. . . .

CONTENTS

Coming in issue number 12!

— *The Reaper* examines Poets of the Eighties. . . .
— Thomas Wilhelmus inspects contemporary fiction. . . .
— The Correspondence column returns. . . .

DON'T BE CAUGHT DEAD WITHOUT READING IT!

No. 11 $2.00

The Reaper is the great deleter, the one who
determines when the story ends. . . .

CONTENTS

Coming in Issue number 13!

— The *Reaper* examines two recent anthologies — Poets of the
  Eighties.
— "Narrative and Awareness," an essay on fiction by Barbara
  Haas . . .
— Poems by Tony Curtis, Chris Semansky, Maurya Simon, and
  others. . . .
— From a verse play by George Keithley. . . .

2

THE REAPER

No. 12 $2.00

Issue 12

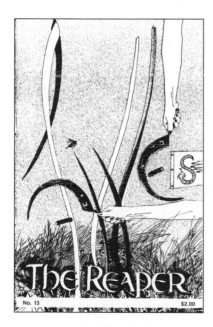

THE REAPER

No. 13 $2.00

Issue 13

The Reaper is the great deleter, the one who
determines when the story ends. . . .

CONTENTS

Coming in issue #14!

— Poems by Frederick Pollack, Robert Peters, Mark Williams,
  Molly Russakoff, John Millett, Jim Cory, Donald Hall,
  Liam Rector . . .

Issue 14

Issue 15

Coming in *The Reaper* 16 "The Death of the Lyric", an essay by The Reaper, plus work by Colette Inez, Dana Gioia, David Wojahn, Jeffrey Skinner, Beth Joselow, Michael Collier, Richard Pflum, Sujata Bhatt, Richard Flynn, Jennifer Atkinson, and others . . .

Editor's note: In the last issue of *The Reaper*, sections three and four of Frederick Pollack's poem, "The Revolution", were accidentally jumbled. They are correctly reprinted in this issue. The editors apologize for the error.

THE REAPER 15

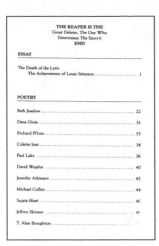

Issue 16

JENNIFER ATKINSON

T. ALAN BROUGHTON

SUJATA BHATT

MICHAEL COLLIER

DANA GIOIA

COLETTE INEZ

BETH JOSELOW

PAUL LAKE

JEFFREY SKINNER

RICHARD PFLUM

DAVID WOJAHN

$2.00

THE REAPER 16

Issue 17

the reaper 17

Issue 18

THE REAPER 18

Meg Schoerke is an Assistant Professor of English at San Francisco State University. She has published poems in journals such as *Triquarterly*, *The American Scholar*, and *River Styx*.